CREDIT WHERE IT'S DUE: THE MONEY DEBATE IN 1930s IRELAND

TADGH QUILL-MANLEY

FIRST PUBLISHED 2022
SECOND EDITION PUBLISHED 2024

© TADGH QUILL-MANLEY

ISBN: 9798825606323

CREDIT WHERE IT'S DUE: THE MONEY DEBATE IN 1930s IRELAND

TADGH QUILL-MANLEY

Credit Where It's Due: The Money Debate in 1930s Ireland

TABLE OF CONTENTS

TOPICAL FIGURES
3
IN THE BEGINNING
9
IS THE SYSTEM AT VAULT?
15
GONNE WITH THE WIND
38
CREDIT WHERE IT'S DUE
62
COLLATERAL DAMAGE?
87
THE CENTRAL BANK ACT
114
CONCLUSION
124
ABOUT THE AUTHOR
126

"They who control the credit of a nation direct the policy of governments and hold in the hollow of their hands the destiny of the people."

<u>The Rt. Hon Reginald McKenna (1863-1943), Chairman of the UK Midlands Bank and Chancellor of the British Exchequer</u>[1]

---

[1] Munson, G. (1944). The Hand That Writes the Credit. *The Kenyon Review*, [online] 6(3), pp.425–454. Available at: https://www.jstor.org/stable/4332530

TOPICAL FIGURES

MAUD GONNE MACBRIDE

ERNEST BLYTHE

SIMON O'DONNGHAILE

TIMOTHY QUILL

Credit Where It's Due: The Money Debate in 1930s Ireland

JOSEPH BRENNAN (CHAIR, CURRENCY COMMISSION AND GOVERNOR OF THE CENTRAL BANK OF IRELAND)

JAMES J. MCELLIGOTT (SECRETARY, DEPARTMENT OF FINANCE)

Credit Where It's Due: The Money Debate in 1930s Ireland

SEAN T. O'KELLY

REV. FR. EDWARD J. CAHILL, SJ

Credit Where It's Due: The Money Debate in 1930s Ireland

PRE-CURRENCY COMMISSION BANK OF IRELAND £5 NOTE (1925)

CURRENCY COMMISSION £50 NOTE (1928)

Credit Where It's Due: The Money Debate in 1930s Ireland

'PLOUGHMAN' £1 BANK NOTE (1937)

CENTRAL BANK OF IRELAND 10 SHILLINGS NOTE (1943)

Credit Where It's Due: The Money Debate in 1930s Ireland

IN THE BEGINNING

When the Irish Free State was founded in the 1920s, the per capita level of income in Ireland compared favourably with that in many post World War I European countries. Ireland also had a relatively advanced banking system that was fully integrated into the sterling area and held ample liquidity in the form of sterling balances. According to Padraig McGowan (of the Institute of Public Administration), one of the main characteristics of membership of the sterling area was the free movement of capital at internationally competitive rates of interest, not only between Ireland and the UK, but also with the rest of the sterling area. Moreover, as far as the countries of the sterling area were concerned, there was free movement of capital from them to the rest of the world.

In the 1920s, British currency notes and coins circulated freely in Ireland, circulated alongside the currency notes and coins issued by the Irish banks and were automatically exchangeable at par with the Irish bank notes, which also did not have legal tender status except during the period 1914-1919. The use of bank cheques and accompanying arrangements for exchanging them and settling the net differences for banks had also been a well-established feature of the Irish banking system from as far back as the 1840s. Therefore, in the 1920s, Ireland had what McGowan describes as a "high efficient cheque-payments system by international standards, both in terms of the costs of cheque transactions and the length of time before they were presented for payment."

This extended not only throughout Ireland, but was also fully integrated into the domestic and international cheque clearing and settlement arrangements of the UK clearing banks. Up to the late 1920s, deposits with the clearing banks (being the banks that provided cheque-payment facilities to their customers) and the savings banks in Ireland were also regarded as being expressed in sterling. When Ireland established an independent state, the authorities were slow to disturb the efficient payments arrangements that existed not only within the country but also for over 90% of the country's international trade and essentially the entirety of its external capital transactions. The authorities were most anxious at the time, hoping to preserve the confidence of the designated non-residents in Northern Ireland and Great Britain, who held bank deposits and saw their real purchasing power increasing in the 1920s. This was especially held in view of the international concern in the early 1920s about the effects of hyper-inflation in continental Europe.

Following careful consideration of the reports of a commission appointed in the Spring of 1926, the government decided in 1927 that it would be in the national interest to effect two significant reforms - the first, to reinstate legally the Irish pound, the other to introduce into circulation a distinctive set of Irish notes and coins. These reforms were to be introduced only on the clear understanding that there would be no exchange controls between Ireland and Great Britain, and that the Saorstát pound would exchange on a one-for-one, no-margins basis with the pound sterling. The Currency Act 1927 declared that the standard unit of value shall be the Saorstát pound, later to be described as the Irish pound in 1937. The Act also prescribed under Section 10 that every contract, etc. effected after the Irish pound came into circulation shall be made in terms of money that is legal tender in the country, unless the contract, etc. is expressed in the currency of another country other than the Irish state. The provisions of the Currency Act became effective in 1928, with the introduction of the Irish legal tender notes and the Irish coinage in substitution for British currency, which continued to circulate freely but without legal underpinning.

The other major reform undertaken in 1927 was to establish institutional arrangements to manage the Irish currency and to ensure that it would continue to be backed 100% by sterling. It was also originally envisaged that the new arrangements would avoid the extension of interest-free credit to Great Britain, which followed automatically from the circulation of British currency in Ireland. The retention in Ireland of British currency for the purposes of effecting domestic payments was equivalent to the holding of British government paper on which no interest or dividend was directly received. McGowan states that it made economic sense to incur the expense of providing Irish currency, since this cost would only be a fraction of the earnings from abroad on the sterling backing for the Irish currency.

The new institutional arrangements to give effect to these reforms led to the establishment of the Currency Commission in 1927. This institution - the forerunner of the Central Bank of Ireland - was made responsible for introducing the newly designed Irish notes and coins in exchange for British currency, which was repatriated. This enabled the Currency Commission to provide a 100% sterling backing for the Irish currency by acquiring sterling assets on which interest was earned. With the introduction of legal tender notes, the clearing banks were no longer permitted to issue their own currency notes, of which there was about £6.5 million in circulation in 1929. In addition, they had to pay interest to the Currency Commission on their notes that remained in circulation. This gave an incentive to the five main banks concerned to withdraw their notes and replace them with legal tender notes. As their currency notes were being withdrawn, each of the clearing banks was permitted to place in circulation a limited amount of quasi private currency notes bearing its own name. These hybrid notes were called Consolidated Bank Notes (however, they were better known colloquially as 'ploughman' notes, as they featured a ploughman on the front) and were provided by the Currency Commission. Despite this, they were not legal tender.

In 1934, a major evaluation of banking in Ireland occurred when a new Banking Commission was appointed, reporting its findings in 1938. This gave the impetus which lead to the establishment of the Central Bank of Ireland in 1942. While central banking was firmly established in most European countries during the preceding century, the worldwide emergence of central banks is mainly a feature of the 20th century and was associated with the international trend towards nationalism and independence.

The Central Bank was made responsible, not only for the functions of the currency commission, but also for the duties and powers conferred on it by the Central Bank Act, 1942. Under this Act, the Central Bank was given the responsibility to guard the purchasing power of the currency and to control credit.[2]

However, many were not happy with the Banking Commission, its conclusions and the subsequent establishment of the Central Bank in the format chosen. Conversely, it also counted many supporters in the public sphere. In this book, we explore the often neglected money debate which rocked Ireland throughout the course of the 1930s, exploring conflicting views and developments through many sources, from mainstream newspapers to the 'radical archives' of various individuals, political groupings and movements.

One of these individuals is Maud Gonne MacBride, the nationalist and suffragist who is often simply remembered as the muse of the famed poet, William Butler ('W.B') Yeats. Gonne spearheaded the campaign for financial reform in order to bring about a form of universal basic income by means of a 'national dividend,' derived from the distributist 'social credit' economic ideology (not to be confused with the communist social ranking points system in the PRC), pioneered by British engineer Clifford Hugh Douglas, and saw control of regional government in Canada (however, today, it is merely a fringe ideology). Gonne sought to have these measures introduced in Ireland for the purposes of eradicating what they labelled 'poverty amidst plenty' and inaugurating an age of leisure. They did so in a general climate of economic stagnation brought about after the 1929 Great

---

[2] McGowan, P. (1990). *Money and Banking in Ireland: Origins, Development, and Future.* Institute of Public Administration.

Depression, as well as economic warfare with our trading partner, Great Britain, across the Irish Sea. Gonne was widely lampooned by social commentators in the 1930s for this suggestion, yet she has since been regarded by UCC's Dr. Gordon Warren as "ahead of the curve in some ways," as the idea of a universal basic income has become a mainstream feature of economic debates in academia and the general public discourse today.[3]

---

[3] Warren, G. (2020). *Maud Gonne and the 1930s' movement for basic income in Ireland.* www.rte.ie. [online]

Credit Where It's Due: The Money Debate in 1930s Ireland

OLD BANK OF IRELAND HEADQUARTERS (NOT TO BE CONFUSED WITH THE CENTRAL BANK OF IRELAND)

IS THE SYSTEM AT VAULT?

The Wall Street Crash and the ensuing Great Depression of the 1930s adversely impacted Ireland, which was further hindered by the 'Economic War,' which took place between it and the UK for most of that decade.[4] The financial system came under attack from several political hues. Maud Gonne MacBride, writing in July 1934, harangued the notion of private finance and debt, penning an article titled 'A World of Destitution because of Usury: The Last Form of Slavery.' Gonne MacBride went as far to criticise the Catholic Bishops for not condemning the financial system in the wake of the Great Depression, despite the system's practices being contradictory to Catholic thought. They lamented the fact that "they only denounce Communism."[5]

On 27th October 1934, the Minister for Finance (Sean MacEntee) announced the appointment of a Commission to examine the banking and credit system in the Free State and "to consider what, if any, changes were necessary or desirable in the interests of the community." The *Irish Press* wrote that "the Commission would engage on a task of the highest importance and responsibility since the services and machinery which are to be the subject of its inquiry form the frame-work upon which our whole economic life rests."

Part of the work of the new Commission would be to review the conclusions of the 1926 Banking Inquiry in the light of subsequent experience. In the interval, many new factors had appeared. The press release continued by stating that:

---

[4] Daly, M.E. (2011). 'The Irish Free State and the Great Depression of the 1930s: the interaction of the global and the local.' *Irish Economic and Social History*, [online] 38, pp.19–36.

[5] *An Phoblacht 28/7/1934*

"the first Commission was appointed in the year after Great Britain had returned to the Gold Standard; greatly alters one aspect of the situation. The regulation of foreign exchanges has becoming increasingly intricate with the adoption of varying standards of value giving rise to new problems. In India and New Zealand, these new conditions have led to steps being taken to set up Central Banking institutions, and similar action is being taken in Canada. The Commission has to consider whether such a Bank is desirable here, and if so to advise on its constitution. Questions of credit connected with the present industrial and agricultural development, the financing of the housing scheme and other social reforms are also to be examined. The Commission is representative of the whole organic life of the people. As well as distinguished economists and men of great knowledge and experience in banking and finance, it will contain men intimate with the economic problems of every section and grade of the community. That personnel assures us that its deliberations will be of enormous value to our people."[6]

On 28 October 1934, W.T Cosgrave, leader of Fine Gael and the opposition in the Dáil, referred to the setting up of the Banking Commission as "the latest public diversion" on part of the government. He claimed that "a consumptive might as well be advised to go to a beauty parlour." They must, he added, mobilise their entire resources "for the purpose of replacing the government by an Irish government appreciative of the needs of the country."[7]

The first sitting of the Government Commission of 'Inquiry into Banking, Currency and Credit,' was held at the Boardroom of the Department of Agriculture on 23 November 1934. Joseph Brennan, Chairman of the Currency Commission, presided. The proceedings

---

[6] *Irish Press 27/10/1934*

[7] *Irish Independent 29/10/1934*

were reportedly private. The Chairman read the Minister's warrant of appointment, which stated that the Commission was to examine and report on the system in Saorstat Eireann of currency, banking credit, public borrowing and lending and the pledging of State credit on behalf of agriculture industry and the social services, and to consider and report what changes, if any, are necessary or desirable to promote the social and economic welfare of the community, and the interests of agriculture and industry. The members of the Commission were; J. Brennan, R.C Barton, Professor J. Busteed, Sean P. Campbell, J.P Colbert, M.J Cooke, Professor G.A Duncan, J.C.M Eason, Lord Glenavy, Professor T.E Gregory, J. Hurson (per Jacobson, Esq.), J.J McElligott, Most Rev. Dr. McNeely, J. Moynihan, Prof. G. O'Brien, W. O'Brien, Professor G. O'Brien, W. O'Brien, P.J O'Loghlin, J. O'Neill and Professor Alfred O'Rahilly. J. McCann took the place of J.M Sweetman.[8]

On 12 December 1934, Fine Gael's General Richard Mulcahy asked the Minister for Finance if he was aware "that the Commission of Inquiry into Banking have decided that they shall meet in private, and that there shall be no immediate publication either of documentary evidence submitted to the Commission or of the reports of proceedings at which oral evidence is tendered by witnesses; and if he will state whether or not a verbatim report of oral evidence will be taken; and if he will make arrangements to supply in confidence to any member of the Oireachtas who may require it a copy of all evidence tendered before the Commission."

MacEntee replied by stating that he had no information regarding the working of the Commission of Inquiry into Banking beyond what is available to the general public. He understood that it was intended (in the absence of an express arrangement to the contrary with witnesses)

---

[8] *Evening Echo 23/11/1934*

that; "all evidence received shall be published in due course in conjunction with the report."⁹

Writing on the new commission in *An Phoblacht*, Maud Gonne MacBride stated that (it perhaps should be noted, ahead of this piece, that Anglophobia and anti-Semitism were commonplace in Irish culture at the time);

> *"Under the heading, A Central Bank for the Free State, the 'Irish Press,' 9th Dec, from Reuters Correspondent, reports that two members of the present Banking Commission, Professor Gregory of England and Dr. Jacobsen of Sweden, are in Basel, Switzerland, to attend a meeting of the Governors of Central Banks, and that Professor Gregory presented a report on the possibilities of creating a Central Bank in Ireland.*
>
> *The Banking Commission appointed by the Fianna Fáil Government is composed of Englishmen and Jews with double foreign nationality and names, who help to make a comfortable bankers' majority on the Commission, which is to report on the most vital issue of whether Ireland is to take control of her own purse or leave it in the hands of foreigners. Does it not strike, even the most thoughtless of plain people, that there is something wrong when two foreigners are sent to report on and seek advice on Irish affairs at an international banking conference?*
>
> *A <u>State Bank</u> is not a <u>Central Bank</u>. A State Bank is the first step to carry out Republican and Old Sinn Fein policy of taking control of our own purse. A Central Bank means handing control of our purse to foreigners."*

---

⁹ *Irish Independent 13/12/1934*

In another article written by Maud Gonne MacBride in the same issue, titled *High Finances for Plain People*, she claims that financial trickery (specifically, what she called 'Trick No.1') was a root cause of the famine and that;

> *"The wizards of high finance decided that Ireland's debt must be forced up to the level of England's debt to justify sound financiers in the name of economy, demanding the amalgamation of the British and Irish Exchequers. The Bank of Ireland superintended this operation, and was made manager of the Public Debt. The plain people of Ireland knew and cared as little in the beginning of the 19th century about the workings of the Bank of Ireland and the forcing up of Ireland's debt which brought the famine of '46, as the plain people knew and cared about the working of Blythe's Banking Commission in 1926, which confirmed the Bank of Ireland in office and anchored our credit to British Sterling, or as the plain people today know and care about the workings of the Banking Commission at present sitting behind closed doors.*
>
> *The plain people didn't or don't know or care, because of Trick No. II, illusion that it is no concern of theirs and that they are incapable of understanding High Finance.*
>
> *I must now repeat, though it be as tedious as a litany, because it is the only way to destroy illusion, that loans from Banks cost the bankers no more than the pay of efficient clerks to write the figured of the lions in their ledgers or the occasional trifling expense of printing paper notes; but that <u>interest</u> on the loans created by the writing in ledgers has to be paid <u>by the people by selling real goods</u>, corn cattle, produce, and that default in the payment of either private loans or taxation for*

the interest and repayment of public loans, entail the seizure of their homes or land or machinery."[10] [11]

On Friday, 4th January 1935, the Free State Commission of Inquiry into Banking, Currency and Credit adjourned until Friday, 18th January. It had been reviewing the facts of the present position of some of the "more important problems" on which it would have to report as a preliminary to hearing evidence from witnesses on these topics. A considerable amount of material had been assembled and surveyed. The Commission requested that persons intending to submit memoranda should do so not later than 31st January 1935.[12]

At the start of the new year, *An Phoblacht* again employed strong rhetoric and proposals in its attitude towards the banking system employed in the country. In a feature article titled *Usury's Trail of Misery*, again penned by Maud Gonne MacBride, and now appealing to the religious faith of potential readers, argued that "usury is the basis and essence of the capitalist system, and the Catholic Church forbids usury.... The crime of usury before the Reformation consisted in the taking of *any* interest for the use of money and not the taking of a greater interest than authorised by law." Quoting the Protestant historian, Lecky, she notes that taking interest from investments such as taking shares in a business, or persons diverting themselves of capital and receiving instead an annual revenue as compensation...

> *"...Is not usury for the capital is not a loan and is not to be repaid. Insurance is also defined. The Monti de Pieta pawn shops now in most countries under direct State or municipal*

---

[10] *An Phoblacht 22/12/1934*

[11] *Nohrnberg, P.C.L. (2011). 'Building Up a Nation Once Again': Irish Masculinity, Violence, and the Cultural Politics of Sports in A Portrait of the Artist as a Young Man and Ulysses. Joyce Studies Annual, 2010(1), pp.99–152. doi:10.1353/joy.2011.0005.*

[12] *Irish Independent 5/1/1935*

control were originally started to counteract the usury of the Jews (again, anti-Semitic views were an ingrained element of Irish culture), *their object being to lend money to poor people without interest, the small sum charged in addition to the loan being for the payment of the officials in charge. So long as no interest is charged on the money loaned, it is not usury.*

We see that the trade in debt and in money, i.e., the medium of exchange of goods, is an illicit trade. It is an ecclesiastical crime and it was made a civil crime also wherever the Church could influence legislation. At one time it was singled out as so heinous an offence that is investigation by torture was permitted. St. Thomas Aquinas with his marvellous clarity, defines the trade in debt and money from trade in all other commodities. 'When therefore a man restores the exact sum he has borrowed, he has done all that is required of him, because to make him pay for usage of this money is to make him pay for a thing that does not exist, or perhaps more correctly to make him pay twice for the same thing and is therefore dishonest.' St. Thomas had seen through conjurors' trick No. I. The creation of millions out of nothing and based on debt, on which, as I showed in previous articles, the Bank of England and the Bank of Ireland were founded. When one remembers that the Bank of Ireland, manager of Ireland's public debt, by building it up to the level of England's debt, and the Bank of England, as central bank by the sudden restriction of credit were responsible for the famine of '46 and its appalling consequences, investigation by torture of such malefactors, hardly would seem exaggerated.

St. Thomas held that all property derived from Usury should be confiscated."

Elsewhere in the feature, Gonne MacBride claims that the current economic system was "enforced on Ireland by Henry VIII, Elizabeth and Cromwell, continued and consolidated by the financial union of 1816." She quotes sections of Pope Pius XI's 1931 encyclical *Quadragesimo anno* in order to 'social proof' her views.[13]

At the meeting of the Court of Proprietors of the Bank of Ireland (BOI), in Dublin, at which its annual report was presented on Friday 25th January 1935, Sir Lingard Goulding, the BOI Governor, stated that "Irish banks were 'banks of deposit,' whose primary function consisted in acting as trustee of the moneys deposited and no evidence could be produced that the banks refused to make sound loans which would be paid within a reasonable time." He made this statement proposing the adoption of the annual report. Continuing, Goulding stated that "the disasters which had befallen American and Continental banks through locking up their funds in other enterprises were, he said, well known."

On the liabilities side deposit, current, and other accounts at £32,130,000, were greater by some £472,000 than the corresponding figure in the previous statement. The report read "under the heading of assets, our cash and money at call, amounting together to £5,255,000, reprint a proportion of 13.8% of our direct liabilities to the public; taken in conjunction with our investments, the ratio works out at no less than 69.8%, pointing to the fact that the Bank's traditional position of strength and liquidity has been well maintained."

Advances to customers, etc, showed a small but gratifying expansion of £155,000. The profit and loss account showed an improvement of upwards of £2,000 over the previous year. Having provided for all contingencies, the net profits amounted to £406,598 which, with the amount brought in from 1934, gave a total of £498,594. Out of this sum, the board proposed that reserves for contingencies be further strengthened by the allocation of £100,000 and the recommended

---

[13] *An Phoblacht 5/1/1935*

payment of a final dividend of 8% less income tax, payable on 1st February, which, with the interim dividend of 6.5% less income tax paid on 1st August 1934, making a total distribution for the full year of 14.5% less income tax, the same as last year. The report elaborated with the statement that "the burden of taxation on the banks had been relieved to some extent by the reduction of 6d in income tax, but there had been no amelioration in either corporation profits tax or in the very severe and unprecedented stamp duty imposed by the Finance Act of 1932 upon their quota of £1,760,000 consolidated bank notes.

The past year had shown a continuance of the unfavourable factors which characterised the previous year. Goulding spoke again on the report, saying "it has proved increasingly difficult to find remunerative employment for our funds in such directions as are permitted to us by our obligations. The problems of the trading community in endeavouring to adjust themselves to present conditions have resulted in some disinclination to borrow, while the difficulties with which the farming community continues to contend have caused us much anxiety."

Reports allegedly indicated further improvement in the trade of Northern Ireland. Referring to the Banking Inquiry, Goulding stated "however much opinions may differ as to whether there is any necessity, or urgency, at the present juncture for a further examination into a system of banking and currency which had been tried and proven, I believe most thinking people will endorse the decision of the Government to include the investigation matters relating to public borrowing and lending, and the pledging of State credit for agricultural, industrial and social purposes. At the moment it is difficult to measure the aggregate amount of national and local public debt, or to make a reliable estimate of the extent to which the country is to be committed in pursuance of the present policy of State-aided enterprise, land purchase and social services that must of necessity prove costly. It is therefore of the highest importance that these questions should be closely investigated, in order that stock may be taken of the position in matters which have such a decisive bearing upon the national finances and the national future."

Reportedly, there had been a further serious decline in the basic industry, agriculture, not yet compensated for by the intense effort to attain a balanced national economy.

"The new policy," Goulding continued:

> *"despite the intricate we of tariffs, quotas, licenses and prohibitions by which it must at present be implemented coupled with extensive programmes of public works and relief schemes, the rapid development of housing and the activities of the Industrial Credit Corporation in raising capital for new enterprises has undoubtedly contributed to a freer circulation of large sums of money, which can hardly have been without a beneficial effect upon the communities in the urban and city areas. Whether such effect can be regarded as a satisfactory off-set to the diminished returns of the general farming population is a question to be pondered. Happily, signs are not wanting that a way out of some of our major difficulties is under discussion. A disturbing feature of present times to which I feel I should refer, is the unsatisfactory financial position in which local authorities are finding themselves owing to non-payment of rates. It is a matter of common knowledge that many of these bodies have become heavily indebted to their bankers by overdrawing their working accounts pending the collection of rates, and in some instances the situation has become so serious that the banks have felt themselves obliged to refuse further advances until some reduction is made in outstanding liabilities. In previous years, the banks were always prepared to finance these bodies to a reasonable extent to tide them over short periods until rates had been collected, but in my view it is against the public*

interest that unlimited facilities for borrowing money should be afforded to local authorities while serious efforts to proceed with collections remain in abeyance."

The motion was seconded by the Deputy Governor, Mr. T. Shannon Martin. Mr. A. Lloyd Blood said that the banking system here was thoroughly sound. If there was any gap to be filled in the system, it should be done by some institution other than the deposit banks. Mr. P.H Grierson said that it was to be hoped that the increase in the stamp duty on bank notes would not become a permanent measure. The report was subsequently adopted.

Meanwhile, the general meeting of the Royal Bank had also taken place on the same day. A final dividend at the rate of 10% per annum less income tax for six months to 31st December 1934, was announced at the meeting. The Chairman, Mr. E. Clive Brooks, said that low rates had prevailed in the money market throughout the year but the directors were satisfied with the Report and Statement of Accounts, although the profits at £48,071 were less than those for the previous year (1933).

The current deposit and other accounts at £6,243,379, which was a decrease of £214,930, as compared with 31st December 1933, did not indicate any contraction of business. As a matter of fact, the opposite was the case as they had a gratifying increase in the number of accounts. Reports from branches, especially country branches, disclosed the fact that the agricultural community had to draw on capital, therefore, their cash balances reflected that state of affairs. Advances to customers on current and other accounts at £3,913,022 showed an increase of £191,559. British and Free State government securities, corporation stocks, bankers' balances, bills discounted and cash at Head Office and branches at £2,927,075 were driven down by the amount of the increase in advances to customers on current and other accounts and the decrease already referred to in current, deposit and other accounts.

It was the opinion of the board that while much had been done by the Government during the past few years in the matter of financing industries by way of making loans not only to existing concerns for capital expenditure, but also to encourage and develop manufacture at home, the success or failure of these enterprises - many as yet in the experimental stage, must depend on their own efforts and the quality and cost of their goods.

"I am of the opinion," Brooks continued, "that in the early stages of operating the Trade Facilities Act, numerous concerns who availed themselves of the Act were handicapped for want of working capital, especially those who were starting manufacturing concerns, as the Act originally was only drafted to provide loans for the purpose of capital expenditure. By the time the factory was organised, the machinery established, the plant brought to the production stage, and the numerous technical difficulties which generally crop up in the early stages of creating a new enterprise overcome, the already slender working capital had disappeared, leaving the company financially embarrassed right from the inception of the business."

He expressed his sympathy with those who had been adversely effected by the economic dispute. The improvement in the state of industry and commerce was overshadowed by the depression in the cattle trade and among the farming community generally. The announcement of the cattle and coal pact acted as a tonic to those who engaged in the cattle trade. He hoped that the year 1935 would see the brining into effect of further agreements beneficial to the whole community. Prosperity in the agricultural industries meant prosperity right through the different interests of the State. It would be but common sense to enter into any economic arrangement which would restore to the country its old unrestricted markets for agricultural products without interfering with its domestic policy of self-development. The report continued that there were other countries which had suffered, and were still suffering, from more acute economic crises than the Free State had

had to face. He thought, therefore, that the country should face the year 1935-36 with a more optimistic outlook.

A vote of thanks was passed to the directors and staff for their work during the past year. W.B Carson and D.R Mack were re-elected directors.

Also on the same day, the Munster & Leinster Bank held their general meeting in Cork. Mr. C. Murphy, presiding, stated that "the profits for the half year amounted to £69,998, £1,106 in excess of those for the previous half year and £2,339 up as compared with those in January 1933. They also included £42,703 from 1933, leaving £112,701 to deal with. It was proposed to pay the usual dividend for the half year of 12% per annum, free of tax; and after transferring £15,000 to Contingencies Account, applying £5,000 in reduction of Premises Account, and placing £5,000 to the Staff Pension Fund, there would remain to be carried over a balance of £42,701.

They attributed the increase in profits to the benefits generally arising from the reduction in the rate of Income Tax. A further reduction of this as well as the removal of the Corporation Profits Tax would be welcomed by the business community. Accounts at £1,596,789, money at call at £1,300,000 and investments mainly in Irish and British Government Stocks at £11,775,664 represented 58.5% of liabilities, including consolidated note issue. £11,862,804 was outstanding in advances and bills discounted. Good returns, they claimed, had been realised for wheat and for the beet crop; but the adverse conditions of the cattle trade still remained. It was, however, hoped that the recent Coal-Cattle Agreement between the Free State and the British Government would give a welcome impetus to this industry, and that in time further extensions of this agreement and of trading facilities in general would be developed between the two countries.

The report and balance sheet were adopted, on the motion of Mr. Murphy, scolded by Sir Stanley Harrington. Mr. J.F Corkeran, P.C, of Blarney, said that they all welcomed the Anglo-Irish trade agreement, and hoped that it would be the forerunner of further action beneficial to business in both countries. In reply to Mr. Hurley, the Chairman said that a director's fee was £500 a year. They used to have five directors, but they now had seven. Hurley said that it was not hair to have increased the fees, especially as the profits of the bank had fallen £46,000 since 1931. The Chairman replied that if Mr. Hurley wanted to raise the question, he could do so by notice. Mr. Collins said that the report and the balance sheet were very satisfactory.

Mr. D. Connor, Cobstown, said that the government had reduced the farmers to poverty. He stated at the meeting that "we are threatened with extermination if we do not do what the book farmers up in Dublin tell us. They have threatened to take the land from them and I've it to the ne'er-do-wells. The cannot be settled by the politicians - they're too well off." He suggested that the senators, deputies, civil servants and road-workers be put into the trenches for one year. After that, they moved onto the election of directors.[14]

In early February, the meeting of a new farmers' organisation in Cork demanded farmers' representation at the Banking Inquiry. The criticised against the Fianna Fáil government's instigation of the economic war regarding the land annuities problem.[15] Only briefly described in the *Evening Echo* newspaper's report, the new organisation was actually arranged in association with the Blueshirts, with the *Blueshirt* organ running a full article on the convention (at which over 500 landowners from across the country were in attendance), where the organisation, named as the 'New Land League' was formed. The organisation sought the "elimination of party politics and the concentration of all on agricultural interests without regard to

---

[14] *Irish Press 26/1/1935*

[15] *Evening Echo 9/2/1935*

political affiliations. It received the endorsement of General Eoin O'Duffy. Mr. E.J Cussen, a delegate speaking on the Banking Commission, stated that;

> *"A most important Commission is now in session, namely, the Banking and Currency Commission, and I have no doubt that the main reason for the setting up of that Commission was to discover ways and means to overcome the difficulties that have arisen as between banks and farmer creditors. Who is in a position to speak with authority on behalf of the farmers of the Free State before this Commission - and I am in a position to say that the Commission is most anxious to hear such evidence?*
>
> *I would particularly ask you to make arrangements today for a representative committee which will submit evidence to the Commission on behalf of the farmers of the Free State, and I hope that the farmers of the Free State will make it possible for that committee to state that they are in a position of authority to appear before the Commission."* [16]

On 22 February, the Saorstat County Councils arranged a memorandum of evidence to bring before the Banking Inquiry. Mr. Thomas Condon, Co. Meath, presided at a special meeting of the County Councils' General Council, held at the offices of the Dublin County Council. The Chairman said that the meeting was called principally on a representation from Wexford regarding the matter of giving evidence before the Banking Commission Other counties were also considering the matter, and it was desirable to have the proposed evidence of the different Councils co-ordinated. A feature of the day, it was claimed, was the reactions on County Council finances to derelict farms due to bank debts. They suggested that through the

---

[16] *The Blueshirt 9/2/1935*

Banking Commission, something might be done in regard to frozen debts.

Mr. McGahan, from Louth, said the matter was one for consideration of a small consultative body rather than a meeting of that kind. The committee could consist of men of long experience in public affairs and the experienced officers of county councils. The memorandum of evidence produced, could, if necessary, be submitted for ratification to a further meeting of that body. The secretary, Mr. Keogh Nolan, said that he had been informed by the Commission that memoranda myst be received before the 31st day of the month. He had communicated with County Secretaries and received memoranda from "two or three" counties. There would be a meeting of the County Secretaries on 5th March, when he thought the question would be considered. A sub-committee was appointed to prepare a memorandum.[17]

The Commission of Inquiry into Banking Currency and Credit held further sessions on Friday 1st of March and Saturday 2nd of March in Dublin, according to a statement by the Government Information Bureau:

> *"On Friday, it heard evidence from Mr. P. F. Walsh, managing director of the Agricultural Credit Corporation Ltd, on the general question of agricultural credit in the Free State and, in particular, on the work of the Corporation in relation thereto. The Commission has fixed 31st March as the final date for the receipt of memoranda from the public, and anticipates that all out standing memoranda will be received during the month, enabling it to make progress in disposing of this part of its inquiry. It had now adjourned to 3rd April, when it proposes to hold sessions on a number of days continuously to hear oral evidence. In the meantime, the Statistical Sub-Committee of the Commission will be engaged*

---

[17] *Irish Examiner 22/2/1935*

Credit Where It's Due: The Money Debate in 1930s Ireland

in the investigation of material required in relation to the inquiry."18

At a meeting of the Standing Committee of the National Agricultural Association in Dublin, during mid-March, with Patrick Belton TD presiding, requisitions from branches of the Association to give evidence before the Banking Commission were considered. It was decided that a memorandum of evidence be prepared by the Policy and Propaganda sub-committee for the next meeting of the Committee. It was directed that a scheme for the liquidation of farmers' bank debts, including mortgages and overdrafts, be prepared as well as a scheme for the provision of loans for farmers at a low rate of interest. Branches and County Executives were requested to furnish evidence as to financial condition and credit requirements for their respective areas. The Standing Committee welcomed the adoption "of portions of our programme by Fine Gael, via-derating and equitable distribution of the burden of the economic war."19

The Commission of Inquiry into Banking, Currency and Credit held sessions during the first week of April. At the opening of the first session, the Chairman reported the progress in the preparation of statistical information by the Statistical Sub-Committee. The Commission heard oral evidence from a number of witnesses in support of written representations previously made to the Commission, and reviewed other memoranda of evidence received. Again, this news was released by the Government Invitation Bureau, indicating to the still private nature of the meetings.[20]

On 16th April, speaking in the original Free State Seanad, Senator Hon. Andrew Jameson on the second reading of the Local Loans Fund

---

[18] *Irish Press 4/3/1935*

[19] *Irish Press 16/3/1935*

[20] *Irish Press 6/4/1935*

Bill, which passed all stages, he said that it was clear that the fund of account was "in a financial mess." To his mind, the Bill gave government a "free hand" in dealing with "all sorts of advances," at the moment, were held for specific purposes. He did not think it was fair that the Minister would have to include in his Budget a certain amount for the assistance that they were going to give in aid of those local loans. Senator Michael Comyn said that these loans had been in "a mess for the last thirty or forty years." An indirect intention of the British parliament in granting the loans had been "to keep the people quiet," and as a result, repayment of the loans was not made at due dates. He knew a case where repayment was said to be statute barred. The Bill contemplated that future accounting and collection would be better. Senator Ernest Blythe said that not the least interesting thing about the Bill was that it should be introduced by the Minister, who, in opposition, said he did not approve of borrowing from the local loans fund and that those loans should be met out of taxation. The provisions seemed to be satisfactory. Senator (and former Labour leader) Tom Johnson said that one of the reason why he was glad that the Bill was likely to become law was because it would provide "a complete disclosure of the accounts of the Local Loans Fund each year."

Senator James Green Douglas asked if there was any possible mix up between the amount of assistance given by way of free grants and the Fund. Were these grants, he asked, included in that Fund?

Speaking on the aims of the Bill, MacEntee said that it was proposed to clear up the position of the sums repaid annually on foot of the loans made prior to 1st April 1922, out of the fund established under the National Debt and Local Loans Act, 1887. The Bill, he claimed, was designed to deal with "the very limited question of the finance and administration of the fund. It did not extend the scope of the fund."

In relation to the Banking Commission, MacEntee referred to Neville Chamberlain's Budget speech in the British Commons and said that after 100 years of experience, the British had come to the conclusion that it was advisable to keep the Local Loans issues separate from the Consolidated Fund. Chamberlain, he said, was taking the opportunity of permitting the issue of local loans stock in a more modern from and of converting the existing stock if the opportunity arose. He further stated that the Bill, in its present form, was provisional. The Government would have to give more consideration to any recommendations the Banking Commission might make in regard to the issue of the local loans and the position of the fund. On the Committee Stage, Senator Patrick Baxter said the Minister should consider whether the Minister should consider whether he should not write down loans in cases where local authorities had incurred liabilities that were difficult to meet. He claimed that "progress was being hindered by the dead weight of debts incurred in the past."

Replying, MacEntee said they "should remember that those loans had been advanced over 21 years ago and at very low rates of interest. They had been advanced to finance housing and sewerage schemes which had brought in a considerable return to the rate-payers" and that he did not think there was a case for writing down. They felt they were still sound loans and were not irrecoverable.[21]

In October 1935, the *United Ireland* newspaper, in criticism of the approach of De Valera's government, ran a section titled *Irish Currency*, which stated that;

> *"The present Government is learning something from its experience in office, though, as we have said before, it is a very slow learner. In some directions, however, it has made more progress than in others, and it is perhaps just as well to take note of such exceptions. One of these is the Government's attitude towards finance and currency. In that connection, the appointment of an Irish Banking Commission in the early*

---

[21] *Irish Press 17/4/1935*

part of this year came as a piece of re-assurance to those whom the Government's political antics had inspired with serious anticipations. The personnel of the Commission was 'calculated to inspire confidence,' to quote the Irish correspondent of the Economist. The Minister for Finance followed up this demonstration of attachment to financial orthodoxy in nominating the Commission by a pronouncement in the Seanad that he did not approve of currency experimentation, nor could he see any hope of betterment in departure from what can be regarded as the canons of finance and of currency orthodoxy. There is no need to anticipate that the findings of the Banking Commission, when its report is ultimately published, will be anything but conservative, though certain changes in our finance and currency system may be recommended. It is a pity, however, that in other directions the Government has not learned to avoid 'experimentation,' and to shun 'any departure from what have to to be regarded as the canons' in matters of ordinary statesmanship and general economics. After more than three years of the economic war, that particular lesson, unfortunately for the country, is still unlearned."[22]

Little more information is available on the content discussed at the Inquiry sessions for the rest of 1935, mainly due to the secretive nature of their operation. In December 1935, Fianna Fáil, the governing party, utilised their Ard-Fheis (annual conference) to mention the money system debate. Eamon de Valera stated that he was "glad that the discussion is warmer in regard to national control of credit - not because the government should be condemned for its action, but because Fianna Fáil is a thinking organisation."

---

[22] *United Ireland 26/10/1935*

He thought it was good that they should all be thinking about "these matters." What he had said at Geneva had been referred to, but he had said nothing at Geneva that he had not said "a hundred times at home." What he had said there was that, as everybody knew, the present system was "not working well."

He continued by stating that "it is easy to point out the defects of a system and say that money could be got for armaments while it could not be got to put people to work - but, who is at fault? Some would say it was the bankers, but I am not sure that are responsible. It is that this is responsible; that fundamentally we are all prepared to make bigger sacrifices to defend the country physically against outside aggression and to preserve its independence than we are to see that our brother is kept alive properly.

I have been shocked to find that it was possible for a large loan to be obtained for a cinema here, while such a loan cannot be got for an industry. Like others, my inclination is to say 'confound the banks and those who control credit in that way.' It is not the banks that are responsible. It is because people will always spend money in cinemas, and because it is certain that the money invested in them will be got back and something more. They should be aware of finding a scapegoat on which to heap sins that do not belong to him. I will remind those interested in credit control that its exponents would themselves say that it was not the banks that were responsible but the present system."

At this stage, it could be observed that Eamon de Valera was willing to defend the private financial institutions that operated in the State. The governing party went on to set out its position in relation to the Banking Inquiry. When the government got the report of the Commission of Inquiry into Banking, they would examine from its own point of view, and with a view to the interest of the community as a whole. The government had, they claimed, shown in the past that it had convictions, and that when a course was for the good of the country they had the courage of their convictions and acted accordingly. In matters of this sort, on which the whole economic system depended, by one "foolish" step they could cause more damage than could be remedied in years. It was obvious that they "must proceed cautiously."

Eamon de Valera stated that "as one who tried to understand the question of credit controlling before it was take up by its present advocates," he would say that he knew of "no method" of monetary control that was going to enable the people of the country to dispose of the surplus bullocks. Behind all this, he claimed, there was a question of direct organisation, and they would have to get a change of heart amongst the people in order that they should realise their obligations to play their part in enabling their neighbours to live. These things had to be done over and above anything that might be done in the way of credit control. He thought, he claimed, it was right that they should have an open mind on the subject, but he wanted to say that there was a problem there that would not be solved by a change in the monetary system.[23]

---

[23] *Irish Press 4/12/1935*

CURRENCY AND BANKING PROBLEMS

COMMISSION OF INQUIRY APPOINTED

MR. MacENTEE'S ANNOUNCEMENT

IMPORTANT QUESTIONS TO BE CONSIDERED

Most Rev. Dr. MacNeely.

THE Minister for Finance (Mr. MacEntee) announces that he has appointed a Commission of Inquiry into Currency and Banking problems in Saorstat Eireann. The terms of reference of the Commission are:—

"To examine and report on the system in Saorstat Eireann of currency, banking, credit, public borrowing and lending, and the pledging of State credit on behalf of agriculture, industry and the social services, and to consider and report what changes, if any, are necessary or desirable to promote the social and economic welfare of the community and the interests of agriculture and industry."

The following persons have accepted the Minister's invitation to act on the Commission:—

Joseph Brennan, Chairman;
Theodor E. Gregory,
Per Jacobsson,
Most Rev. Dr. MacNeely,
Robert C. Barton,
John Busteed,
Sean P. Campbell,
John P. Colbert,
Michael J. Cooke,
George A. Duncan,
John C. M. Eason,
Lord Glenavy,
James Hurson,
James J. McElligott,
John Moynihan,
George O'Brien,
William O'Brien,
Peter J. O'Loghlen,
John O'Neill,
Alfred O'Rahilly,
James M. Sweetman.

WHO'S WHO OF THE MEMBERS

ONE A LONDON PROFESSOR

M. JACOBSSON'S WORK

MR. J. J. BRENNAN, who will act as Chairman of the new Currency and Banking Commission, was Secretary of the Department of Finance from 1923 until the Currency Commission was set up in 1927, when he was appointed Chairman of that body. In 1932 and 1933 he accompanied the Saorstat delegations to the Ottawa Conference and the World Economic Conference in

ANNOUNCEMENT OF THE NEW BANKING COMMISSION IN 1934 (IRISH INDEPENDENT 27/10/1934)

GONNE WITH THE WIND

By 1936, Maud Gonne, famed for her role in the Irish revolutionary period, had advanced her critique of the money system, proposing new ideas, such as becoming an advocate of 'social credit,' the distributist philosophy expounded by engineer-turned economist, Major Clifford Hugh Douglas. Gonne criticised Ernest Blythe's denunciation of social credit economics. Opening an article in the *Irish Independent*, she wrote;

> *"I read with amazement the report of Mr. Blythe's broadcast attack on Social Credit. Major Douglas's contention that production has outstripped distribution with disastrous results of unemployment and starvation, tending to war and anarchy is incontrovertible, and is apparent to all in the desperate scramble for markets, the restriction of output and destruction in almost every country of consumable goods, while millions of people who need these goods are allowed to starve. Major Douglas' remedy, Social Credit, is by means of a National Dividend put purchasing power into the hand of the people to buy the goods, and by a system of discount or price rebate guard against the rise of prices, and for financing these schemes to issue new money through a State Bank, backed by the security of the real wealth of the nation.*
>
> *The contention of social credit is that the State should be run as a business concern. At present, it is the only concern that does not issue a proper balance sheet, as all other business concerns do, showing on the asset side their land, buildings, plant, machinery, etc, on which their business credit is largely based. The State's Budget at present is only a sort of cash account, showing income and expenditure. Irish Social Creditors maintain that the security of what belongs to the Irish nation, Ireland, is a sounder and safer and more tangible asset than British War Loan or British sterling, on*

which Mr. Blythe relies. British sterling is a particularly elusive, undefinable and fluctuating security which in 1927, when Mr. Blythe anchored Irish finances to it, stood at 20/-, but today, outside the British Empire, only stands at 12/- or 11/-."

Concluding her newspaper article, down further, she writes;

"the issue of National Dividend as a birthright to all citizens as shareholders in Ireland as a going concern, to whose capital wealth all their ancestors have contributed, is the simplest and most equitable way of distributing purchasing power to enable the goods that are being produced in abundance to be consumed. As in all properly run business concerns, the size of the dividend must depend on the prosperity of the concern of the nation and its ability to keep up production."[24]

The same month, *The Nation* publication, which appears to have held similar views to *The Blueshirt* in terms of its support for the corporatist system, referenced the Commission in a policy suggestion in a pro-Social Credit (distributist) article in February 1936. Describing Ireland as a "rich country," which was held back by its poorly structured credit system, it called for the repeal of the Free State's Currency Act of 1927, "an act which made Law the suggestions of the Banking Commission, or as the name implies, a Commission of Bankers, whose suggestions, naturally were not adverse to the banking system." Pushing for the utilisation of money for increased production, it slated the U.S Government's Agricultural Assistance Act, which was passed in 1935 by the Roosevelt Administration. The Act, which would be deemed illegal by the U. S Supreme Court, paid American farmers to produce less crops and a

---

[24] *Irish Independent 11/2/1936*

lower general output in all agricultural produce. The article continued that;

> *"It must be painfully clear to everybody that there is not sufficient money in circulation to buy the goods which are being produced in such abundance, and the obvious remedy is to issue enough new money to achieve this object without at the same time either raising the price of goods, or making the new money worthless; the latter of which is called inflation and is the bogey word usually used by the financial interests when arguing against Social Credit."*[25]

At the annual conference of the Irish Trades Union Congress (ICTU), held in August 1936, Tom Johnson spoke on the Banking Inquiry. Referring to the section of the Executive's report dealing with the relations between the banks and the State, he thought that, having regard to the constitution of the Banking Commission, the two representatives of Labour on the Commission would have very little influence on its report. Most of the members directly represented the banks or their interests, and the government. From the history of the majority of the members, he believed that their report would not suggest a departure from the present banking system, but would suggest that the present system would be conserved and the government's commitment constrained.[26]

At the Annual Conference of the Association of Municipal Authorities of Ireland in Tralee, it was reported that new houses built by the local authorities would have to be let by at rents greatly in excess of those previously paid. Many of the tenants were mostly poorly paid workers, and a greta many of them were reported to have been unemployed, and were trying to subside on Unemployment Assistance and Poor Law Relief. The difficulty of paying increased rents out of incomes which

---

[25] *The Nation 1/2/1936*

[26] *Irish Press 8/8/1936*

were already inadequate, or merely the dole, was discussed by the *Irish Freedom* newspaper. It also reported that:

> *"... in many cases to pay rent, at the cost of going short of food. The alternative is not to pay rent. Both things are happening on an extensive scale. Hungry people are to be found in many of the new houses, and the rent arrears are piling up."*

It described a situation where a population would go hungry in an "agricultural country, where farmers have difficulty in finding a market for their produce, and were the output of agricultural produce could be trebled if it could be sold, is a tragic absurdity." It criticised the debt based nature of credit used to build the local authorities houses, arguing that;

> *"the large part of the cost on which rentals are based is not the cost of building, but the cost of providing the money to build the houses, and that the high cost of money is not due to necessity, but to our slavish adherence to monetary practices designed to make profits for the private trade in money."*

In a paragraph titled 'the service of usury,' the article takes a damming increase of the financial arrangements of the country. The writer argues that;

> *"Our present monetary practice has as its principle object, the provision of profitable investments its for the well-to-do, and the poor have to pay toll to the rentier and the money lender, while in thousands of cases their children want for bread. Money was once a commodity and was scarce; now it is a cipher which is artificially kept scarce in order to maintain usury.*

There is no reason why the State should not create money, just as the banks create it, and use it to build houses for the poor without any interest charges whatever, and enable houses to be let at rentals which the poor can afford to pay. There is no difficulty about it; it is entirely practiciable and economically sound.

The real issue involved is whether we in this country are prepared to give first consideration to the service of usury, or to the needs of the poorest and most defenceless of the people. In theory, we say that the people come first, in practice, we let usury rule."[27]

It is clear that the debate on the money system, which was present throughout Europe and America, had cropped up in Ireland. On 16 January 1937, the *Kerryman* newspaper ran an article titled 'Irish Money Controlled by Bank of England: Ireland is an Integral Part of the British Financial Empire.' The article was an aggressively anti - Fianna Fáil in its tone, and unique in its composition in the sense that the subject matter was discussed as a conversation between two 'people,' know as 'Paddy Joe' and 'Shawn Fada' respectively.

Paddy Joe opens the conversation, asking Shawn Fada if he had seen the lecture given by Professor Liam O'Buachalla, M.Comm of University College Galway, at Miltown-Malbay Co.Clare about 'Money, Its Sources and Functions," and was likewise made under the Barrington Trust. Paddy Joe believes it was "somewhat unusual" for the lecture to select a "comparatively small place" in de Valera's constituency to give such a "highbrow lecture."

Shawn Fada, replying, states that "perhaps the Social Credit (the distributist philosophy of Major Clifford Hugh Douglas - not the namesake communist 'brownie points' system in the modern day

---

[27] *Irish Freedom* 1/11/1936

People's Republic of China') heresy is spreading across the Shannon from Kerry into Clare!" The character quotes Professor O'Buachalla as stating that "the acceptance of sterling as a basis for Saorstat currency was, in all the circumstances, wise; indeed, it was the only thing that could be done."

This quote sets up the basis for the (arguably long, by newspaper standards) article. 'Paddy Joe' states that:

> *"surely he knows that 'sterling' is but a boosting name for Bank of England paper. If every time in his lecture mentioned 'sterling' he called it by its real name 'Bank of England paper,' perhaps his Clare audience would begin to get a glimpse of the humour of a Banner County audience, in Dev's own constituency (which is presumably in favour of an Ireland independent of any British control) being solemnly assured by a Galway university lecturer that the acceptance of Bank of England control of Ireland's monetary system was wise and was indeed the only thing that could be done!"*

'Shawn Fada' adds that:

> *"you may think it a humorous situation; I call it pitifully absurd that after the long drawn out tragedy of Ireland's decay under Bank of England rule you could get a Clare audience so unaware of the real cause of Ireland's impoverishment as to be able to listen in patience to a lecture advocating the continuance of that same Bank of England's blighting control of Ireland's money system. Surely Claremen must know as well as the rest of us that no people in all Europe was so impoverished in a land so rich in natural resources while its wealth was drained away into foreign pockets and its children forced to seek a livelihood in foreign lands."*

Paddy Joe:

> "Doubtless they do, but they do not realise that Bank of England control Ireland's money system is possible only because Irish money is based on Bank of England paper, as 'sterling' as is the booster's name for Monty Norman's 'promises to pay' - promises which his bank fulfils by giving you more 'promises to pay the bearer on demand the sum of so-and-so!'"

Shawn Fada:

> "Claremen's sense of humour must have faded out if they can't see the comic absurdity of a Fianna Fáil government, alleged to be Republican, issuing its own paper money on which appears the legend 'I promises to pay the bearer on demand the sum of One Pound (signed by Tralee man, J.J McElligott)' and then when any Irishman tests out this 'promise to pay' he is given a piece of Bank of England paper, boosted as 'sterling' by Professor O'Buachalla. Then, when he reads this sterling piece of paper, he finds that it, too, has the legend 'I promise to pay the bearer on demand the sum of One Pound,' signed K.O Pepplat, Chief Cashier. If he calls on Mr. Pepplatt, thinking maybe he will get gold in fulfilment of this 'promise to pay,' he will soon be disillusioned and maybe thrown out on his ear on the pavement if he starts a row about being refused gold."

Paddy Joe:

> "Since Bank of England paper is at present the basis of the Saorstat's currency, it follows that Ireland's money system is controlled though the Irish banks which all have the Bank of England as their Central Bank. Their holdings of Bank of England paper are therefore holdings of Irish legal tender - in

other words, Monty Norman's paper is legal tender in Republican Clare! But you can get a Clare audience not to burst into laughter at that comic absurdity by continually calling Monty's paper 'sterling.' The magic of words! The annual balance sheets of the Free State banks will be out shortly - just look at them and not the figures of 'cash at the bank of England,' they may also (but probably won't) show the amount of the investments by Free State banks OUTSIDE the Free State - but in any case you can get that from the Government's 'Irish Trade Journal' and it will be eloquent of the 'confidence' of Irish banks in Irish industry, a 'confidence' Prof. O'Buachalla did not refer to in his Ennis lecture."

Shawn Fada:

"But he did tell them at Miltown-Malbay that 'it might not always be advisable to favour our pound backed up by sterling, not is there anything to prevent us cutting away from it, other than the mere question of safety and expediency.'"

Paddy Joe:

"Thanks for nothing! We knew already without waiting for Prof. O'Buachalla to tell us, that 'our pound' (I like his subtle humour in calling the Free State currency OUR pound, when it belongs to the banks and is issued only at their request) is based upon (not merely linked with) sterling since the Cosgrave Government pushed through the Free State Currency Act of 1927 and what one Free State Government did another one can undo. In fact, Mr de Valera's party protested long and loud at the passing of the Currency Act of 1927, which shackled the Irish money system to the Bank of England but, tactically enough, Prof. O'Buachalla didn't refer to that, in Dev's own constituency! What we would've liked him to tell us is exactly why it would, or would not, be

advisable to cut free from Bank of England control and what factors would determine whether it would be safe and expedient. Would Monty Norman hammer the Irish pound just to 'larp us' for trying to escape from his grip? How could Monty depreciate the Irish pound unless he first got hold of huge supplies of Irish pounds to throw on to the market, to 'bear' down the rate of exchange, and how could he get hold of these huge supplies of Irish currency. Would not the exchange vale of the Irish pound depend upon the price-level in Ireland (being of high exchange value if Irish prices were low) and would not the operation of the Price Discount or Just Price technique ensure a low price level and therefore a high exchange value for an independent Social Credit Irish pound?"

Shawn Fada:

"Like most defenders of the bankers, Prof. O'Buachalla prefers not to come town to 'brass tracks.' Instead he indulges in value hints of undefined dangers if we cut free from the Bank of England while he throws a sop to Clare's republican sentiment by reassuring his audience that of course we can get out from under the Norman thumb any time we like - but it might not be expedient!"

Paddy Joe:

"He gave a sort of half hint why he wouldn't thunk such a rebellion against Norman control expedient when he said 'whether we like it or not the great bulk of our trade is done with Great Britain and she in turn, whether she likes it or not, finds she must do a great deal of business with us and sterling is a joint unit of value.'"

Shawn Fada:

"'Joint unit of value' is a good joke - a joke against us! The British pound has hopped up and down in exchange value from 9/9 to 21/5 during the last two decades, and Ireland has not had the least say at any time in the fixing of this 'joint unit of value' The writer of Marketing Notes in the Kerryman has made occasionally acid remarks about the jumpiness of this British-Irish pound, whose exchange value is fixed by Monty Norman through his huge exchange equalisation fund, over which the Free State government hasn't an atom of control. One would set the impression from Prof. O'Buachalla that this very unsteady joint unit of value was fixed by mutual agreement between the British and Irish governments; whereas the fact is that an International Financier controls this so-called joint store of value and is not in any way responsible for what he does to it or how he manipulates it to either the Irish or British government. What Henry Ford said about these International Financiers' unites of blue is still true. Henry Ford said in his book 'My Life and Work' - 'a foot is always 12 inches, but when is a dollar a dollar? If ton weights changed in the coal yard, and peck measures hanged in the grocery, and yard sticks were today 42 inches and tomorrow 33 inches (by some occult process called 'exchange') the people would might soon remedy that.' Henry also said in the same book; "the people must e helped to think naturally about money. They must be told what it is, and what are the possible tricks of the present system, when puts nations and peoples under the control of the few."

Paddy Joe:

"What do you imagine Henry Ford would say of a country which left the sole and entire control of its monetary unit of value in the hands of a power with whom it had been but recently engaged in a life and death struggle, a power from

whose grip it had strive to escape for centuries, a power that had scattered its children over the earth and at one period had left it 'as a corpse on the dissecting table?' But how much greater still would be Henry Ford's amazement if he were told that an Irish Government, of its own free will fastened in 1927 that foreign control on the Irish monetary unit of value; that an opposition party, which vigorously protested at the time against that betrayal, when in power itself did nothing to interfere with that foreign control; and that an Irish university professor could find an approving audience in the very constituency of the leader of that same opposition party to listen to ponderous nonsense about the advantages of that foreign control of its money system."

The article continued for several more paragraphs, and at the end, subscriptions to the National Dividend (part of the Douglas philosophy) League were requested.[28] The *Kerryman* rhetoric was quite strong in comparison to the rest of the media, for more articles debating the money system appeared over the next few weeks retaining the 'Paddy Joe' and 'Shawn Fada' characters. One such article claimed that "we could, if we liked, run our own money system our own way, and pitch Monty Norman to blazes. The pieces also argued for the national dividend.[29] [30] Reduced productive capacity due to a lack of the presence of money was highlighted, with a piece titled 'Think of our 100 Thousand Unemployed - Our Half Used Fields and Factories; Our Thousands of Emigrants - The Days of Hand Labour are Gone - This is the 20th Century, the Age of Power Machines.' This was a clear reference to the argued inability of the State's economy to meet its full productive capacity due to a lack of

---

[28] *Kerryman 16/1/1937*

[29] *Kerryman 23/1/1937*

[30] *Kerryman 30/1/1937*

money in circulation in many areas, causing a lack of employment and reduced incomes to boost consumer spending (a demand side view).[31] Two and a half years into its existence, the Commission maintained a private profile during its sessions, hidden from the public. In early February 1937, Labour TD Mr. James Everett asked the Minister for Finance whether the Commission of Inquiry into Banking and Currency had furnished their report to him, and if whether it was intended to publish the report at an early date. The Minister had to reply by saying that he had not yet received the Commission's report.[32] That same month, an article by Seamus G. O'Kelly in *Labour News*, taking the 18th century United Irishman, James Hope, as inspiration, quoted his views on finance, stating that;

> *"Commerce, freed from unnecessary restrictions and established on social justice, would furnish in abundance all the commodities necessary to a people and abolish usury and the concentration of a nation's wealth in the hands of a few great capitalists."[33]*

Meanwhile, as the population waited for an outcome, the *Kerryman* pushed on with a pro - distributist, social credit agenda, featuring an article titled 'Social Credit As Solution to Gaeltacht Problem.' The article read;

> *"the Chairman of the Munster & Leinster Bank, Sir Stanley Harrington, made a very interesting speech, announcing the usual 12% dividend, free of tax. Marvellous how year after year, slump on boom, they can manage to hit that 12 percent bull's eye. This 12% is paid after putting aside £68,727 for possible bad debts, which is added to £43,257 put aside last*

---

[31] *Kerryman 13/2/1937*

[32] *Evening Echo 3/2/1937*

[33] *Labour News 6/2/1937*

> *year for the same purpose, making £111,984 in all. Are they getting ready for that slump forecast for 1940? In addition, £15,000 was put aside for the Contingencies Account (these worrying unforeseen contingencies). £5,000 was put aside for reduction of Premises Account (depreciations), another £5,000 was put aside for Staff Pensions Fund, and even then £41,918 was carried forward to next year as a mere balance in hand. Add up all the sums, 'put aside' and work out what dividend on the paid up capital they could have issued if they used up all their admitted profits! The paid up capital on 31 December, 1936 was £750,000 - there you are. Roddy the Rover, how about that for a problem for your pupils, to prove how prosperous we are. But even the Chairman grumbled at the Note Duty Tax of 2% to the Currency Commission."*

The tit-bit of the speech came later. Referring to the Bank's aspects, the Chairman mentioned that cash in hand and money at call, plus investments, amounted to some £15 million. This sum, he noted, "is equivalent to over 61% of our total obligations to the public." Therefore, even including investments, the Bank could only cover 61% of its depositors' claims—assuming there was time to sell the investments for cash, provided there was no general rush to sell that would crash prices, and assuming buyers could be found. Buyers tend to become suspicious when too many investments flood the market. But here was the real titbit, he claimed. The Chairman continued, stating, "And again I would like to mention that the bank's investments, if taken at current prices today, represent a considerably larger sum than that at which they appear in our balance sheet, thus constituting a valuable reserve."

He pointed out that Social Creditors often talked about the bank's hidden reserves. The banks, with their profits, bought up stocks and shares and then grossly undervalued these investments in their published balance sheets. This, he said, was sound finance—not placing too high a valuation on assets. However, he questioned how hiding swollen profits from public scrutiny helped to maintain "a strong liquid position." He wondered how the Corporation Profits Tax law stood in this regard. Why should the utmost penny of tax be squeezed out of the little man, who couldn't lighten his tax burden by investing part of his wage or salary because he had to spend it to live, while wealthy corporations could hide their real profits by investing the lesser part as available for dividends? Major Douglas had informed the people of New Zealand about the enormous hidden reserves of the New Zealand Banks, but this revelation was not exclusive to those banks. It also applied to the banks of green Erin, whose investments were mainly outside the country, with the credit they claimed as theirs to monetise as they saw fit. He wondered if Mr. 'Sound Finance' MacEntee might cast an inquisitive eye on those hidden bank profits when drawing up his next Budget. Perhaps he felt safer squeezing the little man, who, after all, could always be depended on to respond to appeals for "sacrifices in the cause of freedom."

He also mentioned that his Kerryman colleague, 'Tomas,' had provided readers with a fascinating account in *Cursal na Seachthaine* the previous February, detailing the genesis of Peig Sayers' diary, which he judged to be as welcome an addition to contemporary Gaelic literature as *An t-Oileánach* or *Fiche Bliain ag Fás.* That was high praise, and it made him all the more surprised that no reference had been made to the tragedy of financial poverty that was quickly turning the "well of Gaelic undefiled," An Blascaod Mór, into a wasted, empty island. Had he not seen that terribly pathetic letter which poor Muiris Ó Súilleabháin himself had written to the press, pleading for a little money to help the last few islanders stay, and begging for leniency to keep the island school open, even though only twelve scholars were attending it? The "averages" injustice had raised its sound financial head on the island as menacingly as elsewhere. The school had probably been closed by now, and the teacher departed. He lamented how wholeheartedly and efficiently the fight to revive the Irish language was managed. The only hope of saving it from fading away into a mere school-time, schoolbook language was to concentrate on the all-too-few areas where it was still a living tongue. In An Blascaod Mór, its vitality had burst into the bloom of living literature. Yet, for want of a few figures in a banker's ledger, or a few thousand of the ten-a-penny currency notes that the Currency Commission's printer could produce in a few hours, the Blasket fishermen saw their thriving industry snatched from their hands by foreigners, and family by family, they were forced to emigrate. He questioned whether Gaelic Leaguers were blind to the connection between a false, unchristian money system that imposed unnecessary poverty on the Gaeltacht areas and the decay of the Irish language happening before their very eyes. How, in the name of common sense, could the Irish language be preserved unless the men, women, and children for whom it was truly their vigorous mother tongue were enabled to live and prosper, to increase and multiply? He asked what was needed to enable them to prosper but an adequate supply of those tickets for goods called money, to save Irish manufactures from the already threatening menace of "over-production." There was plenty of work to be done in the Gaeltacht areas and plenty of men eager to do it—but where, oh where, was the money to come from? As he was on the verge of bursting into unprintable language, he decided to shut down on this tragic subject of the dying Gaeltacht, but he left with this parting arrow: the Gaelic Leaguer who was not a hot, uncompromising, and aggressive claimant for the issue of the National Dividend was a shortsighted fumbler who imagined Irish would live even as the Gael disappeared.

This article is signed off by 'E. Ua Curnain,' followed by an appeal for people to join the National Dividend League, located at 2 Upper Ely Place, Dublin.[34] Ua Curnain was a regular contributor to the *Kerryman* and was a hardened advocate for the introduction of Douglas' distributist philosophy as a prerequisite for the establishment of a truly independent, 'Gaelic Irish Catholic State.' He questioned what he described as bankers' "monopoly of the money

---

[34] *Kerryman* 27/2/1937

system."[35] He juxtaposed the *Kerryman* against the "city dailies" as a publication that was more in tune with 'ordinary people.'[36] Debate was sparked further in Kerry by advocates of the Douglas philosophy following the referendum on the adoption of the new Constitution of the State. The lecture was titled 'The New Constitution and the Money System,' which was given by Mr. T. Kennedy, of Dublin, secretary of the Social Credit Bureau in Ireland. They met at the Old County Hall in Tralee. Proceeding, Kennedy stated that the improvement of the well-being of the people was the fundamental test of all forms of government. He claimed that the new constitution would ignore the necessity for changing the present financial system and that the well-being of the greatest number would not be improved and may become even worse. He said that any system of political government which ignored the vital importance of first, national control of national credit, and, secondly, that such national control shall promote the equitable distribution of all goods and services up to their technical ability to supply them, such as political system of government would fail to serve its people as they should, he claimed, be served.

He stated that after the revolutions in Ireland, that the right of the Irish people to govern themselves must be recognised, but without national control of national credit, such self-government was impossible, be the political form of government what it may. Kennedy continued by saying that to understand the importance of national control of national credit, the population ought to understand the fundamental facts of the present money system. It is generally not understood, he believed, how powerful the control of credit is; yet, when they realise that the power to create and to destroy money is inherent in such control; that such control governs price levels and thus determines how much of every other commodity we must produce in exchange for a given number of money tickets, it must be obvious how powerful and far-reaching such control of credit can be. He re-iterated the points of

---

[35] *Kerryman 13/3/1937*

[36] *Kerryman 27/3/1937*

Ua Curnain that the Bank of England "governs the price of every egg in Ireland."

Taking the Rt. Hon. R. McKenna's definition of money as including "all forms of currency, together with bank deposits readily withdrawable by cheque," the population would soon realise that the great bulk of our money is created by banks writing figures in their books. Kennedy elaborated by saying that:

> *"currency represents less than 1% of the huge total sum which annually passes through the London Bankers' Clearing House, the enormous balance being made up of cheques and promises to pay, which effect the exchanging of the great bulk of the goods produced. This creation of money has been summarised most effectively by McKenna in one of his many interesting addresses to the shareholders of the Midland Bank, when he stated; 'the amount of money in existence varies only with the action of the deposits. We know how this is effected. Every bank loan and every bank purchase of securities creates a deposit, and every re-payment of a bank loan and every bank sale destroys one.' The MacMillan Banking Commission Report of 1931 (at which Douglas testified), page 34, fully describes the process of lending which creates this astonishing result.*
>
> *The financial credit to which banks thus give expression and embody forth, does not belong to them. It obviously belongs to the whole community, past and present, who create it. We have, however, allowed a tiny fraction of the community, the bankers, to annex it; to decide who shall have it; to charge for its use and all this without being responsible to the community in any way for the consequences of their dealings in what has ben described as 'the economic life blood of the nation.' The consequences of such un-coordinated issues of money is fully*

realised where coinage is concerned, the right to issue, which is one for he most jealously guarded emblems of sovereignty.

We inflict the savage sentence of three years' penal servitude on anyone who is found guilty of issuing four 'bad' half-crowns, but we allow individuals to create and destroy hundreds of thousands of pounds every day without holding them responsible for the consequences of their actions, wielding, as they do, more and more control over the lives of their fellow citizens. As a result of the present financial procedure, money is almost invariably kept short in quantity; there is no method whereby the quantity of money and the prices of the goods offered for sale are kept level and commerce is reduced to an ignoble scramble for a share of these insufficient money tickets. The symbol does not accurately represent the things symbolised."

Kennedy went on to advocate for an Irish State Bank and that the controls necessary would not be enabled by instituting a Central Bank alone, which he believed could "might easily be a satellite of the Bank of England, or worse still, that of the Bank of International Settlements in Switzerland." A distributist philosophy, he emphasised, was essential for the practical realisation of some of the principal teachings of the Christian religion. It would combat poverty, which he stated was "a breeding ground or Communism" and that "the cure for communism was to remove poverty which was increasing." The ideas which he had put before the audience were, he thought, were "the very finest antidotes to communism."

Proposing a vote of thanks to the lecturer, Dr. Michael O'Connor, Listowel, said that there were 29 central banks all over the world, each of which was under the control of the bank for International Settlements in Basle. He sincerely hoped that the Free State would not set up the thirtieth central bank following the report of the Banking Commission. He compared the Bank for International Settlements to an octopus with its tentacles spread out through 29 different countries. Speaking at the CYMS (Catholic Young Mens' Society) rally in the Albert Hall, London, Rev. Owen Dudley said; "let us demand that more money shall be made and that human life shall come before the money system. It is bread that matters, not paper. It is the people that matter, not the Bank of England."[37]

In the run up to the 1937 general election, the Labour Party did not hold back in its rhetoric on a strong condemnation of private finance. In a two page spread of the party programme in a June issue, the programme's subheading is titled 'Put Real Human Interest Before the Exactions of Financiers!' In the final section of the party's proposals, the following statement is given;

> *"It is objected that the cost of the proposals outlined by the Labour Party is too great to bear within the current financial structure of the State, the Labour Party answers that, as the reforms enumerated in this programme are absolutely essential for the well-being of the community, the financial structure of the state must be altered to meet the needs of the people."*

Concluding, the closing cry spells out, in capital letters; "ALL WHO BELIEVE THAT THE CLAIMS OF HUMANITY MUST TAKE PRECEDENCE OVER THE EXACTIONS OF FINANCIERS WILL ENDORSE THIS PROGRAMME AND VOTE FIRST FOR THE LABOUR CANDIDATES."[38]

In September 1937, an article titled 'How Banks Lend the Nation Its Own Credit,' was featured in *Labour News*, having been penned by Mr. Michael J. Keating. He argued that;

---

[37] *Kerryman 24/4/1937*

[38] *Labour News - 19/6/1937*

> *"the fact is that every State is in debt, and must remain permanently in debt to the Financial System. The result is subservience to the permanent credits and means, in cold fact, GOVERNMENT BY BANKERS. That is the position in cold, sober fact as it is today, and as it will continue to be until changed, and only the people can change it. Under it, no progress, no national up-building can take place without the permission of those who control the nation's money supply."*

Keating also complained that "we agitate for nationalisation of transport, for municipalisation of bus and tram-way service, but what about the nationalisation of money?" He also cites Pope Pius XI in order to support his agreement for national control of money. Keating wrote that;

> *"In his Encyclical 'Quadragessimo Anno,' his Holiness the Pope describes money and credit as 'the life-blood to the entire economic body' and points out through its agency 'immense power and economic determination are concentrated in the hands of the few men who grasp in their hands the very soul of production, so that no-one can breathe against their will.' Is this power and despotic domination to continue, polluting the economic life of the community at its very source, sacrificing human life and human happiness to the greed for gain and power, or is this 'immense power' to be, in the words of the Pope, 'brought under the effective control of the public authority'? That is for YOU to say, and you will need to get ready to say it louder than the Banking Commission which will soon be telling you that the 'Free' State owes much to the sound conservative policy of its Banks. It does. It owes to that policy its slums, its under-nourished rickety children, its thousands of unemployed, its high cost of living, and a thousand and one other modern evils."*

However, Keating also points the responsibility of bringing about the changes necessary to the electorate. Making an impassioned plea as he closes his article, he says;

> *"But it owes these evils just as much to the ignorance and stupidity of the people, who permit business companies, called Banks, to control and treat the nation's credit as if it belonged to them, and who are prepared to go cap in hand to the Banks for the kind permission to use the credit, which belongs to the people, promising not only to repay it, but to pay a tribute for being allowed its use. O Tempora! O Mores!, which being interpreted means: are we mad, or just plain stupid?"*[39]

Later, news broke in October 1937 that the report of the Commission of Inquiry into Currency and Banking, set up three years earlier, was being prepared and according to a "well informed authority" writing in the *Dublin Press*, may be ready in "a few months."

A source revealed that the principal report of the Commission would stress the fact that, regardless of any potential changes in world conditions, agricultural production and the sale of agricultural products at the best possible prices had to remain the mainstay of the Saorstát economy. The Commission saw no objection to supporting agriculture with loans, provided that farmers had a reasonable opportunity to earn income to repay those loans. They further considered the level of indebtedness related to land to be comparatively low.

The Commission, it was understood, had noticed a tendency to belittle agriculture in favour of small factories scattered across the country. They believed that mass thinking in the Saorstát had shifted towards a demand for more industry, while in almost every other European country, agricultural development was emphasised with a deep

---

[39] *Labour News 18/9/1937*

understanding of its value. The report was set to emphasize the paramount need to maintain and strengthen the position of the farmer and the farmyard, considering them the true factories on which the country must place its real reliance. Speaking on the accounts, the source stated that;

> *"the Commission has been noting this also and the fact that the adverse balance is becoming lager. It was over the £20,000,000 mark in August. Whilst making allowance for capital expenditure, the belief is that the problem of paying for imports in relation to the value of our exports is becoming more onerous than it had been, and is something the consequences of which must be carefully watched and considered by those in authority. With regard to industry, the Commission is not opposed to development on sound lines, but the wisdom of the far flung high tariff system is questioned. The conclusion appears to have been arrived at, that after beer and spirits and to a lesser extent, biscuits, the export of manufactured commodities, whilst important, was comparatively negligible in relation to the national economy. That this condition of affairs would continue to exist is accepted as the basis of the industrial position here. The major industry of the country, agriculture, and the community as a whole, must therefore, it is concluded, be prepared to ear a considerable burden so that manufacturing production amongst new industries on a limited scale, for the home market may be contained."* [40]

Calling for a separate currency in a later article that year, E. Ua Curnain claimed that the distributist moment in Ireland "quote in support of their endeavours to tell the people the truth about the banks' creation and destruction of money - not by a long chalk. There is economist R.H Hawtrey, Asst. Secretary to the British Treasury, for

---

[40] *Southern Star 9/10/1937*

Credit Where It's Due: The Money Debate in 1930s Ireland

LABOUR PROMOTES SWEDISH MODEL FOR IRELAND (LABOUR NEWS 6/2/1937)

instances, who bluntly stated 'the banker creates the means of payment out of nothing'; there is the Report of the Macmillan Commission of Enquiry into Banking and Currency; there is the Encyclopaedia Britannica, Hartley Withers and J.M Keynes, Professor Stanley Jevons and Professor Frederick Soddy - and many more."[41]

---

[41] *Kerryman 13/11/1937*

CREDIT WHERE IT'S DUE

In February 1938, *Labour News*, Labour's latest reconstituted organ, criticised the Minister for Finance, Sean MacEntee, in a front page article, writing that;

> *"Forty months after constituting a Banking Commission to report on the difficulties of currency and credit, he has no report and no information! The journal of the Institute of Bankers, in October, 1935, said; 'The Commission may, perhaps, appear rather cumbrous in regard to size, but this is compensated for by the very representative character of its membership, which should be sufficient to inspire confidence that hasty decisions will not be arrived at, nor changes of a revolutionary nature proposed... No mention is made in the terms of reference to the establishment of a Central Bank... As regards currency, it need not seriously be feared that a body of the type chosen will do anything to endanger the all-important interest in the Free State's foreign exchange position for which economic expediency alone dictates the preservation of the link existing between the Saorstat pound and Sterling..."* [42]

The hardline newspaper *Prison Bars*, discussing evictions through an article fuelled with emotive language in June 1938, quoted Seamus Lennon, a member of the first "Republican Dail" in 1919, on the potential eviction of a Co. Carlow based widow by the name of Mrs. O'Rourke, along with her five young children, from their farm due to an impending bank foreclosure. Lennon claimed that;

> *"According to Divine Law, Mrs. O'Rourke owes not a penny to the Bank. In all probability, the Bank owes her a considerable sum in the usury interest paid all these years (the*

---

[42] *Labour News 12/2/1938*

debt was contracted in the years of the World War, when banks were offering loans to everybody, inflection was then the policy of the Bank of England, making money cheap). He went on to say how the Banking Commission, set up by England after the War, reduced the currency in Ireland from thirty-three millions to eighteen millions, then to nine millions and the so-called Irish Banking Commission reduced it still further to six millions in 1927, thus robbing the people of twenty-seven millions (because, the Bank of England was, after the War, following a policy of deflation - making money dear).

It is probable that Mrs. O'Rourke never heard of the Banking Commission, or inflation and deflation. She just worked, trying to stave off the seizure of her farm, wondering why each year she had to give more and more farm produce to pay the same debt 'till she had not enough left to feed her children and no more to give the Bank - so her farm is claimed by the Bank and she is evicted - a typical case."

The article went on to claim that there were "thousands of such cases which the money-controlled papers don't report" and that "this will go on as long as we have not an Irish Government ready to take this control of credit from the Bank of England and use it for the benefit of the Irish people."[43]

Later in the same month, another hardline, self-described "Separatist" newspaper, the *Republican Review*, carried an article arguing that British influence over finance in Ireland could lead the latter country into a conflict involving the former (e.g what would a year later become World War II). The contributor, only credited as 'J.P.M,' claims that;

---

[43] *Prison Bars 1/6/1938*

> *"It surely follows, too, that our new industrial financial 'line-up' with England if anything makes it more certain than ever that we shall become involved in England's wars. It is bad enough to be put into the position of being liable to attack because of our close connection with and importance to England. What must be thought of arrangements that actually commit us to conflicts fought with imperial expansion. There is at present in Ireland among quondam Republicans a great deal of talk: 'England will be obliged to protect Ireland in her own interest.' That is a servile attitude. It needs, too, but little for such people to make England's causes their own in any circumstances, especially if in the light of the Banking Commission report a Central Bank, subsidiary, not in form or outward showing, but in real fact, be set up to gather together to one centre the financial web that already entangles us. And such a central bank is already foreshadowed."*

Ending the article, the writer claims that "we must conclude, therefore, that in spite of protests, and above and beyond the powerful influence that a new oligarchy exercises in our Irish life, the final centre to which we may trace the raison d'être of modern Irish Free State industry is the interest of British financiers and the needs of Imperial defence."[44]

The Banking Report of 1938, which wished to restrain the money supply, was used as an authoritative source by the ideologically aligned Fine Gael party. In August 1938, the party claimed that the Report indicated in a very definite manner that the stand of the 'Cosgrave Government' and the Fine Gael party was the only programme consistent with financial stability and security, according to T.F Higgins, at a Fine Gael executive meeting in Portlaoise. He argued that the "mad orgy of expenditure" of borrowed money which had, he

---

[44] *Republican Review 23/6/1938*

said, created an appearance of wealth in recent years had been exposed in its "true colours." The task of retrenchment and the recapture of ground lost through political recklessness would not be an easy one, but it was a task which should be faced by the Government without consideration for political expediency.[45]

In September 1938, former Labour TD, Timothy Quill, publicly presented 'Labour's Social Outlook,' the party's revamped policy, which he had created. The final section dealt with the 'Money System,' of which he stated;

> *"We have been hearing a lot in reference to the report recently published of the Banking Commission, and in the majority report there is a very clever suggestion or recommendation that a Central Bank be formed in Eire in order to co-ordinate the Banking system here, but the real object is, of course, to bring the money system of this country under the control of the international money system. It may be of interest in this connection to point out that since the end of the Great War, twenty nine Central Banks have been established in twenty nine different countries. Each of these central banks being entirely outside the control of the government of the countries, but every one of them are affiliated to the Bank of International Settlements in Switzerland, of which Mr. Montague Norman, Chairman of the Bank of England, is a direct with Dr. Schaet and Rothchild as co-directors. This Bank has a stranglehold on most countries today through such Central Banks, and it would suit admirably the Bankers and Banking Commission if our Government were to establish a central bank here.*
>
> *I wish to say a few words about loans for carrying out public works. Some six years ago in my town, over 100 houses were*

---

[45] *Irish Press 15/8/1938*

built for poor people who lived in slum dwellings. The loan for this purpose is carrying an interest rate of 5.75 percent, plus one thirty-fifth of the principal to be paid each year. Now, the rent charged for these houses is sufficient to pay the whole financial cost in a little over 31 years, but at the end of this period, the occupiers will not own one square inch of the houses of which they have paid the cost. Now, I am not taking interest charges into account, because I believe that loans issued for housing needs and such purposes should be issued by the State free of interest charges. I think I saw where the New Zealand Labour government, through their Bank, are issuing over three million pounds sterling free of interest. If New Zealand can do it, why not Eire?

What is physically possible is financially possible. This is a slogan that should be made known all over the land. We have the men, we have the materials, all we are short of is the money tickets to enable us to get all the work done, afforestation, housing, land reclamation, schools, drainage, etc. There is nothing to stop doing all these things that would make out country a nation worth living in. Nothing to stop us but foreign control of our money system and we cannot do these things until we remove this foreign control and take over full control of our money, so that we can use an Irish credit for the benefit of the Irish people."

Endorsing the document, Maud Gonne MacBride said that she was pleased that Quill had "stressed the historical side of our problems." She also agreed that until the money question was dealt with by the Government, the country's many problems could not be tackled satisfactorily. She suggested that if people were to consider the destruction of France and Germany during the Great War, and what had been done to repair the damage, was there any reason why an Irish Government should not have dealt with the slums during the past eighteen years? Gonne suggested that the document be produced in pamphlet form.[46] Reporting on Quill's document, the *Sunday Independent* stated how it described Labour's financial policy, by which banking and credit would be made a State function, so that "the credit of the country would be used to benefit all the people."[47]

At a meeting of the Cork Co. Committee of Agriculture in January 1939, those in attendance discussed with Rev. Fr. Hayes on the Dairy Shorthorn Breeders' Congress. Fr. Hayes deplored the "flight of the people of the land." The wonder was, D.L O'Gorman said, the flight was not greater because "the farmer was skinned." He was not left "a shilling for himself." The Banking Commission report stated that per head, the Free State was higher taxed than any comparable country to be found. On a population of less than three millions the income from taxation, national and local, including concealed taxation, was about £41 million.[48] That same month, at the AGM of the Federation of Irish Manufacturers, Mr. J.J Walsh, president, dealing with the report of the Banking Commission, said that national manufacturers would not be greatly disturbed by the suggestion that the Industrial Credit Corporation's powers should be restricted because "few purely Irish concerns had been helped." In the then present instance, when investors were nervous it was vital from the point of view of confidence that some system of industrial financing should again be devised by the Government if many industries giving a great deal of employment were to be retained. In the matter of maintenance or alteration of their currency system, they were, he claimed, "not of one mind." At the moment, he believed, there was no doubt that the majority would stand firmly for the viewpoint in the Majority Report of the Commission.

---

[46] *Kerryman 10/9/1938*

[47] *Sunday Independent 4/9/1938*

[48] *Evening Echo 7/1/1939*

Whether they liked it or not, he added, the fact was that development of any kind likely to give additional employment "just now has ceased." Even where money was urgently needed to sustain existing employment that was not available. He submitted that there was no single factor in the present stagnation more accountable for this unfortunate state of affairs than the precipitancy of the Prices Commission in prices examinations, which had succeeded in "frightening the man who alone was capable of creating and sustaining employment."[49]

At a meeting of the General Court of the Bank of Ireland, the Governor, H.B Pollock, said that the end of the Anglo-Irish economic war was regarded as heralding the birth of a new era in the relations between the two countries. He stated that:

> *"another feature of the year was the publication of the report of the Banking Commission, whose deliberations had occupied a period of over three years. The report is an admirable work, covering a vast field of enquiry into banking, currency and kindred subjects in Eire. The valuable nature of the volume is much enhanced by the inclusion of an excellent analytical table of contents of the majority report which facilitates study and ready reverence in a remarkable way. Everyone concerned in the preparation and production of the report is deserving of the highest commendation.*
>
> *In so far as the Irish banks are concerned, it is noteworthy that no substantial changes in the banking system are recommended. On the contrary, the report goes as far to prove that the interests of the public have been well served by the banks and that the system in its existing form is admirably suited to the particular requirements of our country. References in the majority report to the high degree of*

---

[49] *Irish Press* 18/1/1939

prudence and skill with which the Irish banks conduct their operations must be a source of satisfaction to shareholders and management alike."[50]

The annual general meeting of the Provincial Bank of Ireland Ltd was held at the Head Office of the Bank, 8 Throgmorton Avenue, London E.C. 2, with the Chairman, Mr. Richard Durant Trotter, presiding. The other directors present were; Hon. David Francis Brand, Mr. John Charles Denton Carlisle, the Hon. Sir William Henry Goschen K.B.E, Mr. Henry Samuel Howard Guinness and Mr. Alexander Brodrick Leslie Melville. The Secretary was Mr. George A. Kennedy. Speaking on the Banking Inquiry, they claimed that it represented "a most valuable contribution to the study of banking credit, public borrowing, and allied questions. They noted the bank's role in developing joint-stock banking in Ireland from 1823 onwards, which was recognised by the Commission. The Commission found that the three prime objectives of monetary policy should be the maintenance of exchange stability, the establishment of sound credit conditions and the maintenance of a relatively stable price structure. They claimed that the report "concludes that these three objects can best be achieved by the retention of the Eire pound at the existing parity with sterling - a conclusion which has given widespread satisfaction. In the sphere of banking, the Commission concluded that the banks in Eire were conducted with a high degree of prudence and skill, and that there was an adequate supply of commercial credit at favourable rates."

They noted that the Commission recommended some enlargement fo the powers of the Currency Commission, and also suggested that it name should be altered to indicate that the monetary authority of Eire was a central banking organisation. Among the subjects which the commission gave great attention were those of State borrowing and lending, also the growing indebtedness of local authorities. These

---

[50] *Evening Echo 20/1/1939*

recommendations, they believed, should prove the very great value, at that time, when borrowing for housing purposes has become "somewhat of a problem for local authorities. The difficulties in dealing with the problem, they claimed, were enhanced by the high cost of building and the failure to let the houses when built at 'economic rents.'

Discussing the State's trade balance, the Chairman noted that he referred to infrequently the trade balance of Eire. The Banking Commission stressed the importance of not allowing the accumulated external assets to be impaired by a recurring annual deficiency in the balance of payments. Such assets, which he believed it "wisely" pointed out, were one of the greatest safeguards of the financial independence of the country and make it possible to avoid even in a critical period appealing to foreign financial markets for assistance. The net sterling assets of the Irish banks reached the lowest point yet recorded in the Autumn of 1938. One of the principal causes of this decline was, he claimed, the raising and transfer to the United Kingdom of the proceeds of the Financial Agreement Loan of £10,000,000 sterling. However, he believed that the end of the Anglo-Irish economic war had improved the economic landscape.[51]

The private banking institutions were generally happy with the outcome of the report. According to Maurice Moynihan, secretary to the Government and later governor of the central bank, before the report was published, "among some bankers, also, there lingered a feeling that the government and parliament now exercising jurisdiction from Dublin were, in some degree, on probation and that a monetary authority subject to their control might be under pressure to stray from the traditional paths of financial prudence."

The majority report signed by Brennan, its chief author, and 16 members, exceeded 350,000 words. Three minority reports ran to

---

[51] *Irish Independent 26/1/1939*

60,000 words. Two volumes of minutes of evidence came close to 1,500 pages. The principal finding was simply to leave things as they were. The system of banking and currency was fine. The link with sterling was "the only possible policy." Before the Banking Commission reported the new Constitution to which Moynihan contributed had been enacted in 1937. Included in Article 45, the Directive Principles of Social Policy which are for the guidance of the Oireachtas, is the following: "in what pertains to the control of credit the constant and predominant aim shall be the welfare of the people as a whole."[52]

Writing on unemployment, E. Ua Curnain noted "the growing demand for national ownership of the nation's credit," and praised the 'Standard,' rejuvenated as an organ of the workers of social justice. Condemning 'Roddy the Rover,' of the 'Irish Press' (owned by Fianna Fáil) for castigating it, he claimed that the "cheap jeer at the workers for social justice is something to gladden the hearts of the communists and all others who work for intensification of the Class War." Ua Curnain criticised his praise for the present system, declaring that:

> *"let our 103,000 unemployed and their dependents answer; let our emigration figures and our marriage rate answer. Let the debt of National and Local debt, the merciless taxation of our people (soon to be intensified by the coming move to increase assessments) in the interest of Bank domination, and the shameless robbery of the poorest amongst our people by the 'Sound Finance' inflation of rising prices - let these nationwide facts answer."*

Furthermore, he wrote that "reasoned criticism, stimulating reasoned debate is welcome and serves a useful purpose. The cheap jeer at the demand for social justice serves only the enemies of Ireland. Ua Curnain criticised calls for higher taxes by 'Roddy the Rover' in the

---

[52] *Irish Times 24/11/2014*

'Irish Press,' asking "perhaps Roddy doesn't know that taxes are not required for the purpose of enabling the Government to pay its servants? The bankers kindly create the money necessary in the first place (using paper and ink to monetise the Irish nation's credit), lend it to the Government (so long as they think the Government is worthy of such favours); and Roddy's 'patriot chiefs' then proceed to use all the various measures of the taxation system, including the Flying Squads to squeeze enough money out of the people to repay the bankers. To realise the audacious fraud of the taxation system, maintained by Roddy's heroes, note well that the money created from paper and in in the first place by the bankers, and lent to the Government, morally belongs to the Irish people. It belongs to the Irish people morally because the Irish goods and Irish services which alone give that money its value were provided by the Irish people and not by the bankers. Even Roddy, in the intervals between his periods of patriotic palms and eloquent Dempseyisms, may have noticed that bankers do not plough and sow or reap and mow; neither do they tend the sick or teach the ignorant or build houses or transport goods.

One day, please God, this moral right of the Irish people to their own credit will be given legal recognition and actualised in an Irish State Bank. For that day the new 'Standard' is working, Its argument is the mildly-moderate conservative case put forward by Mr Peter J. O'Loghlin in Minority Report No. III, whose main attraction for me is contained in its proposal that the Currency Commission should create (not borrow) the money necessary to put the Irish unemployed to work at drainage schemes, afforestation, land reclamation, etc. I would work with any man whose endeavour is to break the Debt grip of International Finance on the economic life of the Irish people, and for that reason I would urge Irish Social Creditors to support the new 'Standard.'

It is great to note that the call of this endeavour has overleaped all political barriers (Ua Curnain cites an alleged example of proof of a plan to slow down the 'Irish Industrial Revival'). Roddy rounded off his little jeer at the workers for social justice by stating 'they (the patriot leaders) cannot change the laws of nature which decree that man must toil and suffer and can prosper only by industry and thrift. Yet unable to work miracles but labouring ever in anxious zeal they have achieved this much that the free part of our country has more frugal prosperity more contentment within it than almost any other land in Europe.'"

Ua Curnain returns from this quote by writing "the number of our registered unemployed is now some 103,000 and the 'decree that man must toil' seems to have missed them! They suffer alright, on the 'frugal prosperity' of the dole fixed by Roddy's patriot chiefs (like the other 'social services'), at a figure too mean to even support a Minister's greyhound."[53]

At the 1939 AGM of Galway County Council at the end of January of that year, Mr. J.J Cunningham moved the following motion on the agenda;

> *"that we urge on the Administration that they might continue to manifest, instead of a narrow capitalistic economic timidity and conservatism which in many States is fast becoming anachronistic, a versatility in conception and development that obviously had been their programme prior to the publication of the findings of the Banking Commission. That the development of our State resources and needs even if limited to schemes of an economically reproductive character demand, instead of a retrenchment, an increase in expenditure based, if necessary, on the social credit economic theory."*

The chairman, Mr. E. Corbett, suggested that before this motion was discussed, the embers be supplied with dictionaries. Cunningham said that he appreciated the disposition of the members and the laugh that

---

[53] *Kerry News 30/1/1939*

the motion had raised, but he suggested that the time was very opportune for a discussion on this question. This motion applied to the findings of the Banking Commission, but he did not propose to argue it from a subjective point of view. He was, he claimed, merely anxious that the Government be asked to do something to implement the report and this motion, and he was apprehensive that there might be a difficulty to the fulfilment of the programme following the report of the Banking Commission. They had in the modern world, he claimed, a position where countries which owned nine-tenths of the world's gold were faced with want in the midst of potential plenty. Mr. O'Donohoe MCC agreed. Continuing, Cunningham argued that;

> *"we take the biggest countries in the world to which this applies. Take Germany, England, France, Italy, America and Russia and we find that as regards these countries there is a policy of what we might call silence. A recent event has borne out my theory and has thrown the world of finance in chaos. That was the dismissal by Herr Hitler of the President of the Banking Commission in Germany. If you read the various newspapers that commented on that motion, you will find that my motion is as nothing at all in comparison to the criticism of those papers. The dismissed official was necessarily hostile to the system of the wholesale provision of money."*

At the stage, the members were talking amongst themselves loudly and did not appear to be taking any interest in Cunningham's arguments. It was therefore very difficult for the journalist to hear the speaker who held the floor. Cunningham then turned to the body of the council chamber and remarked "I have not the least intention of sitting down until I have fully explained my motion." An adjournment motion was put to the council and carried.[54]

---

[54] *Connacht Sentinel* 31/1/1939

In January 1939, the *Wolfe Tone Weekly* castigated the banks' approach to funding local authority housing schemes (going as far as to accuse Sean MacEntee of being complicit in their approach), claiming that "an interesting extension of the bankers' money racket is about to take place." Continuing, the article reads;

> *"The city of Dublin is now mortgaged to the banks to the limit of the capacity of the people to bear the burden of repayment of loans plus interest (i.e usury) charges. A re-valuation of the city was foreshadowed by 'Sound-finance Mac Entee' a short time ago, not of course, on his own initiative. The banks just told him, and he did as he was told."*

The publication claimed that the banking institutions had previously "sabotaged" the Dublin Corporation's housing schemes by refusing to finance them, and their representatives on the Banking Commission "provided them with the excuse," and that the government had acquiesced in their destruction of local government "in direct contradiction to the papal encyclicals." Arguing that banks "have no use for houses as such, they are merely pegs on which to hang up a debt and usury," the "net result of all this financial huggermugger is that those who actually produced the houses are deprived of the ownership of them, which rests with the banks."[55]

In February 1939, further extracts from the **Banking Commission Minority Report No. III** were released on a large scale basis for publication in the press;

> *"I do not believe that it is wise to emulate the ostrich and to bury our heads in the sand, and refuse to face the grave social issues raised by the Papal encyclicals, and indeed the scanty treatment these issues have received in the Minority Report is a matter which I view with equal surprise and regret. I desire*

---

[55] *Wolfe Tone Weekly 28/1/1939*

to emphasise the gravity of the evils which urgently require economics remedy, for they constitute a danger to national security. Continuous and widespread unemployment has led through the pressure of economic necessity, to emigration on a scale unparalleled since the years following the famine, Ireland is still a food-exporting country, as it was in the famine; moreover, our country possesses great undeveloped resources for the production of the necessities of life; yet multitudes of families, both in the country districts and in the towns, are forced by preventible economic causes to live on or below the line of bare subsistence. The condition of affairs that is frequently glossed over by the term 'Social Problem' in plain words means semi-starvation to a very large number of families, and the grave malnutrition of children. In spite of mass emigration, the number of our unemployed remains more or less constant. About 90,000 of our citizens drag out an existence on the miserable pittance of unemployment assistance. I stress the fact that this denial of the constitutional right of citizens to obtain an adequate means of livelihood through their occupations is creating a new submerged class, below even the level of the propertyless proletariat. Furthermore, the steady dwindling of the rural and agricultural population, and a marriage rate that is the lowest recorded in the world, taken together, constitute a menace to the national safety of Ireland that will be immediately obvious. The signatories to the Majority Report may have been able to ignore these vital issues; but Ireland cannot ignore them and remain a nation.*

I therefore feel compelled to raise three questions which I regard as being fundamental in our inquiry. They are:

1. *Will the present monetary system, even with the adjustments which have been recommended in the Majority Report, enable the Irish community to use the economic resources of the*

nation to the full extent required to provide a sufficiently high standard of living for the whole population and in particular to use the whole resources of available labour?

2. *Will the present monetary system permit of the growth of a social order based on justice?*

3. *What changes (if any) in the monetary system would facilitate the orderly transition to a condition of full employment, and towards an order based on social justice.*

The considerations I have already advanced combine with the terms of reference to oblige me to consider, first of all, how the national economic activity can provide all citizens with the means to live by their labour.

The general tenor of the Majority Report leads to the conclusion that it is neither the business, nor is it within the power of the Government, to make effective provision to secure and maintain a condition of full employment. We are warned against attempted being made to allow social contributions to interfere with what is assumed to be the unalterable working of economic laws. The idea that it necessary to conform to unnamed economic laws which operate with predetermined precision, whatever the social consequences may be, is one from which I dissent completely. I think that economic policy should be made to meet human needs, and not vice versa. I cannot accept the position that, if the financial system fails to enable a condition of full employment to be reached, the unemployed must therefore be left in penury, dependent on public or private charity, or compelled to emigrate in order to live. I believe that the financial system exists to serve the community and not that the needs of the community must be fit down to fit the Procrustean head of the banking system as it exists today.

Credit Where It's Due: The Money Debate in 1930s Ireland

Throughout the entire period of the political union with England, Ireland was subjected to a financial union which operated with disastrous effect on the Irish economy. The facts are too much a matter of common knowledge to need repetition here. Partly as a deliberate policy, and partly through sheer neglect of Irish interests, this country was unable to share in the industrial growth common to other European nations in the nineteenth century, but remained merely a source of supply for food and cheap labour for England. In this disastrous period, the Irish population fell by approximately 50%, at a time when the population of every other European race was increasing.

The first few years of self government after 1921 brought no economic change. Apart from an outstanding electrical development, there was little industrial growth. Emigration, which the war had stopped, quickly reappeared on an extensive scale. The fiscal union continued unaffected by the political changes which had taken place.

The integration of the Irish economy with the fiscal and economic system of Great Britain has been and remains inimical to the major interests of the country. In this no question of politics is involved: it is a matter of economic facts. The major economic, and indeed, national interest of the Irish community is to have a prosperous agriculture. The census of 1926 showed that there were 1,233,000 in the twenty-six counties engaged in various occupations...

The fiscal and economic policy of Great Britain is destructive of an agricultural economy. It has aimed principally at manufacturing goods for export, the marketing of these goods abroad, and the imposing of raw materials and food. As a part of this policy, there has been a vast investment of British funds in other countries, and this has not only served to finance further export trade, but the hope of securing a return on their foreign investments depended on the continued investment of further sums and a continuance of export trade on an extended scale.

This system is not, and was never suited to Irish needs. It imposes on us the policy of another country in whose development we are unable to share. British policy has consistently disregarded the interests of agriculture at home and left it exposed to the competition of other countries in order to get cheap imported food for the industrial towns. British agriculture decided in the nineteenth century and step by step with it Irish agriculture also declined. Agriculture was sacrificed in England in order to facilitate a profitable business of manufacturing and exporting goods. Agriculture was sacrificed in Ireland as a necessary consequence of Ireland's economic and fiscal union with England. We shared in all the losses and in few of the gains, or at that period we were without choice.

The European war brought the decline of agriculture to a halt for a few years, but in the post-war period it was resumed. In England, although some measure of protection has been recently given to agriculture, and large sums have been spent on subsidies and State-aided marketing schemes, the decay of agriculture has not been arrested...

In Ireland, the decline of the rural population has been continuous for nearly a century, and in spite of all the measures taken by the Irish Government in recent years, both in encouraging the development of industry and in protecting and subsidising agriculture, emigration continues and is on the increase. Taking the returns of the passenger movement by sea as providing an indication, however, incomplete and inadequate, of this movement, we find an excess of the numbers of passengers leaving Saorstat ports... It is evident that the decline is of a very alarming character, and appears to be increasing at a rate which, if continued, will precipitate a national disaster comparable only to the results of the famine of 1846-1848, unless prompt and effective measures are taken to deal with the situation. From even so cursory a review as the foregoing, I reach the conclusion that English economic and fiscal policy has been consistently destructive of the economy based on agriculture: that agriculture both in England and Ireland has in the past been sacrificial to other interests, and that the assumption which runs through much of the Majority Report that the effect of keeping Irish monetary policy in step with English policy will be of benefit to this country, is not only not proven, but on the contrary, is completely at variance with the facts disclosed by the economic history of Ireland since 1800...

So far from holding that the present depressing trends should be accepted as the hypotheses, on which future economic and monetary policy should be not to take for granted undesirable trends, but to change them and to guide and turn them to the national advantage. If we are to accept emigration and a falling population as something inevitable, and base future policy on such a hypothesis, then it follows that the national economy will suffer a progressive and fatal contraction... There can be no doubt that the population problems is the most important of the questions which come within the scope of economic science. Man is the end as well as the means of all economic activity; and the number of inhabitants is the most important factor which determines, on the one hand, the volume of the output of wealth, and, on the other hand, the abundance of enjoyment in any nation, or in the world as a whole. One might have expected, therefore, that the Majority Report would have addressed itself to the consideration of what changes in monetary policy might serve to prevent the progressive decline of the Irish nation, rather than that it should use the fact of a present decline merely as an argument for the careful limitation of public expenditure. No more fitting common on the neglect of vital issues has been expressed than that of Professor George O'Brien when he wrote:

> *'This is unquestionably the major economic problem of the age, and it is curious that so many economists are content to fiddle on monetary, financial and banking problems when the Rome of all economic activity, mankind itself, is beginning to burn away, possibly to extinction... No scheme of agricultural or industrial development or of public investment can claim to have been adequately considered if regard has not been had to the probable future population. The planning of economic life of the country in other directions is obviously futile if this most vital element is left out of account. Politicians in the Free State are generally protectionist and interventionist in outlook; but on the central economic problem of all, the numbers of people, they are apparently apostles of almost complete laissez faire. The danger of such inconsistency is that the present generation may be making sacrifices to build a structure that there will be nobody to enjoy, forgetting the saying of Pericles, that what makes a city great is not its walls, but its men. - ('The Coming Crisis of Population,' in 'Studies,' Dec 1935).'*

It is a fact beyond question that the monetary policy which is pursued in any country can and does in a great measure determine the extent of economic activity, as well as the degree of economic security which may be enjoyed by its people. It is also, I think, beyond question that the almost universal economic insecurity now felt by every class in the community is a major factor making for a decline in the population...

I repeat that, in my view, it is the first function of monetary and economic policy not to accept, but actively to combat, such conditions and to devise means to bring about a condition of full employment of all our resources of labour, in order to secure a livelihood for himself and his family in his country. If this is done, emigration would practically cease, unemployment and the fear of unemployment would disappear, standards of living would rise; earlier marriages would be possible, and a general feeling of security would permit of that atmosphere of confidence and hope, which alone will reverse the rapid decay which has overtaken the country...[56]

The matter of the extension of credit to local government has seemingly caused tensions in the wake of the commission. At a meeting of the Dublin Corporation (now Dublin City Council) on 6 February 1939, Mr. J.J Byrne said that "the time has come when the people have got to be told that, credit-worthy as the Corporation was, the banks no longer would co-operate with us. The burden of housing is a national problem and should be a national charge. The report of the Banking Commission has sounded the doom of housing, and the time has come when every man will have to take his stand either behind the banks or behind the people."[57]

Two days later, on 8 February 1939, the *Irish Independent* revealed the decline in the net external assets of the banks. The net figure for the final quarter of 1939 stood at £61,387,318, as compared with £82,982,785 for the corresponding quarter in 1933. Decreases in other external assets were revealed in the report of the Banking

---

[56] *The Liberator (Tralee) 4/2/1939*

[57] *Irish Independent 7/2/1939*

Commission. The article stated that "no doubt there probably was a repatriation of money for the purpose of home investment, but not on a sufficient scale to account for the decrease of £21,595,467."

Referring to the balance of payments, the Banking Commission found that in each of the years 1929 to 1936, there had been an adverse balance on the current account which had to be covered "either by encroachment on external capital assets or by increase of external liabilities." The newspaper continued that "so far as external capital assets are encroached upon to cover the adverse balance, there is a loss of external income which, in the words of the report, 'increases the difficulty for the future of bringing the current account of the balance of payments into equilibrium and tends to make the country more dependent upon the maintenance of its export trade.' This view has evidently made an impression on the Minister for Finance, who, in a recent statement, admitted that the country should become more dependent upon the sale of agricultural products abroad to make good the increasing deficiency in the income from external investments. The problem is how to make up for the set back to the agricultural industry within the past six years. Last year, an increase in the value of agricultural exports was recorded; but it was due more to higher prices than to a larger volume of trade. If dependent has to be placed more and more upon agricultural exports, it is manifest that production must be increased."[58]

In a Dail debate on that same day, Sean Lemass (FF), Minister for Industry and Commerce, moved the second stage of the Trade Loans (Guarantee) Bill. He said that the powers granted under the 1933 Bill expired on June 1st 1938 and this Bill purposed to revive the power to grant loans. The majority report of the Banking Commission had recommended, he said, the repeal of the Trade Loans system on the ground that the high rate of loss to the Exchequer made State machinery undesirable, and that the system resulted in the

---

[58] *Irish Independent 8/2/1939*

Government having a direct financial interest in industries the success or failure of which might be largely dependent on the exercise of Ministerial powers, which would be "a source of embarrassment."

General Richard Mulcahy (FG), pointed out that Lemass was recommending the continuance of a policy which the Banking Commission had regulated against. He stated that "the Minister's estimate of only a £13,000 loss on the loans since 1933 was fantastic in the light of what some of us know." J.L Esmonde (FG), welcomed the Bill in so far as it was an attempt to provide employment in the future. He would "like to see some limitation whereby Irish money advanced or guaranteed would be in the hands of Irish citizens and would not be under the control of those from outside."

However, Dublin City councillor and TD, Patrick Belton (FG) clashed with Fianna Fáil proposals on industrial development. He claimed that industry had been made bankrupt by Government policy over the course of the last six years and thought that the House should be slow in doing something the financial experts of the Banking Commission had advised against. Lemass, in reply to criticisms levelled against him, claimed that the prospect of losses under present Government policy was considerably reduced and that was a fact that the Banking Commission did not take into account. He believed that the Commission's proposals were unconvincing.[59] [60]

Speaking on the FF government's Valuation Bill the following day, opposition leader W.T Cosgrave (FG) argued in the context of agriculture that there was now general agreement if they were to prosper they must export agricultural goods or some goods that they would have to sell in the foreign markets. Those things they used to hear about self-sufficiency had gone by the board. They had to get money from some source. As their investments outside were

---

[59] *Irish Independent 9/2/1939*

[60] *Cork Examiner 9/2/1939*

diminishing, it was important that their exports was the cost of production. Everything that militated against production in this country, he claimed, was going to prevent them getting in the money which they must have. The sims of money paid by the Government to local authorities for property of which they were in occupation had increased from £7,800 in 1930-31 to £115,000 in 1938. That was one of the matter which the members of the Banking Commission had in mind when they drew attention to the rising cost of local as well as national administration. Another clause of the measure, he stated, would leave it open to the Commissioner of Valuation not to bother about Government property. The measure seemed to provide, he added, every possible facility for the Government and its various departments to get whatever information they want, and to impose penalties on individuals who did not give that information.[61]

---

[61] *Cork Examiner 10/2/1939*

Credit Where It's Due: The Money Debate in 1930s Ireland

IN 1938, THE BANKING COMMISSION REJECTED THE IRISH TRADES UNION CONGRESS' PROPOSAL OF PUBLIC OWNERSHIP & CONTROL OF CREDIT (IRISH PRESS 8/8/1938)

COLLATERAL DAMAGE?

Meanwhile, back in Galway, J.J Cunningham addressed the motion he had put forward at a meeting of Galway County Council to the readers of the *Connacht Tribune*. He stated to them that;

> *"As I cannot accept as entirely correct your report of my elaboration of my motion at the meeting of the Co. Council on the 28th last, you might kindly facilitate me, as the most effective means of making the necessary corrections, by publication of my prepared speech in total. The following is substantially my speech, representing as I have ascertained by informal discussions with well-informed people, a not inconsiderable volume of opinion on the subject: Let me commence by saying that this notion of motion in no way insinuates any lapse in the fulfilment of these programmes of development and of social amelioration by the administration, nor to imply any want of confidence on the part of the mover in their ability and intention to continue to implement the programme. It simply means that they might find fulfilment of it more difficult because of the tenor of the findings of the Banking Commission - a tenor inimical to the increase in the necessary expenditure, even for schemes of a reproductive character. There is, I observe, a disposition on the part of some of the members to jest about this motion, to demonstrate, I take it, their own felicitous superiority to the witless mover. I wish them joy of their self gratulations, but I would remind them that oratorical or literary dialects might not alway spring from grandiloquent or vainglorious notions - that they might sometimes be opposite because of the dramatic appeal and intrigue they are calculated to create.*
>
> *Of course, I do realise that his motion might be more adapted to another forum than the County Council. It would almost certainly be so were it intended to argue the motion from a*

> *merely subject point of view. But that is not contemplated. It is intended to apply it to the current concerns of the Council to the delay on the part of the Department of Local Government and Public Health in sanctioning loans applied for by this Council very many months ago, and to warn the members of the Council about the economic irreconcilability that must always obtain in circumstances of a retrenchment of expenditure by the State in the development of rural resources and needs side by side with the constantly increasing demands of rates and taxation. But the mentalities of some people do not appear adequate to appreciating that such a problem confronts this country.*[62]

It is perhaps easy to see through the nature of Cunningham's language, where his disappointment and anger at his fellow council members' disinterest and/or unwillingness to grasp what he regarded to be the issue of their generation is clearly visible. This is perhaps best emulated in the section where he states his belief that the county council is probably not the best place to discuss the debate on the money system at the time, although the importance he believed it had on its operation and its ability to fulfil its role as a government is omnipresent.

Writing on matters pertaining to the Department of Finance, the *Irish Independent* reported on the estimates for Supply Services for the year 1939, which were in the process of being prepared. It said that the salient future of the public finance of Eire was, as stated by the Banking Commission, the large and continuous growth which had been taking place for many years in both State and local expenditure, both on revenue and loan account, in taxation and public debt. A computation which had been made for the commission of the total disbursements within the State of national and local authorities, including revenue and loan accounts, showing that the total

---

[62] *Connacht Tribune 11/2/1939*

expenditure had jumped from £31,852,000 in 1931 to £43,204,000 in 1936. In the same period, the sums raised from the community through taxes and rates had risen from £26,872,000 to £32,180,000.

In 1937-38, the expenditure on Supply Services was £27,760,088, as compared with £20,775,341 in 1930-31. For 1939, the estimate for these services was £30,322,710. The newspaper reminded its readers that in 1930-31, provision had to be made in these estimates for large disbursements which had in recent years disappeared. These included £1,150,000 in respect of local loans and £1,834,000 payments to the British Government. The amount raised by taxation was £21,005,000 in 1930-31, but in 1937-38, although the Exchequer then reaped the benefit of half the withheld land purchase annuities. Over and above the revealed taxes the citizens had to bear heavy charges in the shape of hidden taxation, because the extent of these charges was not set out in the Budget, the *Irish Independent* had maintained that the official returns did not give a full disclosure of the real toll exacted by the Government from the community. Referring to the amount raised through tax rates and taxes in 1936, the Banking Commission observed that the figure did not include "the considerable amount of latent taxation entailed by the sugar monopoly nor the burdens placed on the consumer by the State action affecting the prices of flour and certain other commodities." After what was described as an "exhaustive investigation" of the position, the Commission came to the conclusion that "there has been a marked deterioration recent years in the state of public finance." In view of that serious verdict, the newspaper proclaimed that "it is incumbent on the Minister for Finance and the Government to reduce the taxation which oppresses every individual and every industry."[63]

The publication of further extracts from Minority Report No. III, by Mr. Peter O'Loughlin to the Irish Banking Commission, were

---

[63] *Irish Independent 14/2/1939*

disseminated in the press. O'Loughlin proclaimed that "preventible poverty is cramping the lives of our people" and that;

> *"the assumption that this connection (between Ireland and Great Britain), do advantageous to one country and so disastrous to the other, will undoubtedly continue for an indefinite period, contains the implication that Irish autonomy will be exercised in the political field alone, but will not be exercised in the direction of developing a national monetary policy of our own. The statement that nothing is clearer in monetary science than the debility of having uniformity of currency and monetary usage between different countries, is, I fear, more interesting as a commentary on the type of monetary and economic theorising which sometimes passes current for economic science, than it is useful of valid as a guide for an Irish monetary policy. It should not be difficult to see that the monetary policy which it is desirable to pursue in any particular country and depend on the particular circumstances of that country, and just as the historical development, the degree of industrialisation and the economic resources and aptitudes of the various countries are different, so the monetary policy which is capable of meeting their separate needs is likely to differ also."* [64]

Discussing the matter of rates, the *Donegal Democrat* ran a feature, saying that;

> *"in Donegal we want lower rates this year and in the words of one Councillor who seems actively opposed to it demand that we are 'fed up' with ever increasing rates. If the Councillors, who are showing themselves responsive to public opinion, will give us lower rates without cutting down on any country works or our having any increase in general taxation, we will*

---

[64] *Kerryman 25/2/1939*

be perfectly satisfied with whatever method is adopted. All we can say is that we are convinced that it can be done and we do not want to be paying twice over for county works that we should not have to pay for even once. We do not want to go deeply into the money question, but we have pointed out already the paragraphs in the Majority Banking Commission Report where it is grudgingly admitted that banks can and do create money. The same admission was contained in the official Banking Journal recently in England. To create means to make from nothing.

There seems to be no limit to the amount banks can create and lend at a high rate of interest according to the supporters of the present system and there is no harm done to anyone by such creation, but good. Why, therefore, can the Government not create money similarly and advance it to County Councils free of interest? This is the big WHY which must be answered. It is not for the Donegal people to put forward arguments, but for those who hesitate to support the demand to give sober reasons why they cannot do so. But there is more in all this than lower rates. The agitation raises much larger question of whether or not the will of the people is to prevail in Government, or in other words whether it is a 'democracy' or a 'hypocrisy' we are to have in this country. We are told by the weekend papers that, despite the universal protests against the Re-valuation Bill, the 'machine' majority of the Fianna Fáil party will ensure its becoming law. The Donegal County Council, by an almost unanimous vote, representing accurately the sentiments of the electors as a whole throughout the county, condemned this Bill and yet our Fianna Fáil TDs must, when the Party Whip is cracked, and even though they hate doing it, vote to make this hateful Bill into law. Any man who calls that democracy is an unblushing liar.

A favourite plan of this undemocratic 'scarcity in the middle of plenty' system of Government we now are beginning to see unmasked, is, when any section of he community shows signs of being crushed too far, to relieve them at the expense of the rest of the 'scarcity' sufferers in the community, instead of relieving them out of the abundance that could be called into being by a sensible national money system, a system such as enabled by Franco, though he had no gold, to beat the Spanish Reds with all the gold, or Dr. Salazar to build up Portugal. For instance, private motor lorries are going to be sacrificed in the interests of railways. If this is allowed, it is an injustice to and an infringement on the liberties of a large section of the public and at the same time there will be no real or serious benefits of railways, which will never prosper until the rest of the country begins to prosper and the boys and girls are able to stay at home.

Then again, we expect very soon loud trumpeting about 'derating' and great ceremony will be made about this concession to farmers and they will be expected to complain no more. The rest of the community will be saddled with the burden and it will soon find its way on to the farmers' backs again in the shape of increased prices, etc. Take one item, flour, our staple food, which is roughly twice as dear here as in the Six Counties and calculate how much the farmer with wide, and say, six children, pays on it in the year more than he should pay. And this is only one of the necessities of life. What are his rates compared with the sum he overpays in flour and other necessities during the year?

The whole money system is obviously out of gear and exercising a hampering effect on the whole country. And yet our dons are so conservative that they would rather go on talking and talking and considering until there is an explosion rather than admit what is an obvious fact and raise their voices and demand forthwith the remedy and so speak for the relief of the poor who cannot speak for themselves.[65]

At a meeting of the Waterford Chamber in late February of 1939, several representatives of Waterford business, including the Mayor, Mr James Aylward, complained of the increased taxation faced by the area since its revaluation in 1924-26. Mr AJ Phelan, B.L agreed with the suggestion that the taxable limits of the country had almost been reached, and said if they got down to bedrock, they would find that the lot of apparent prosperity did not actually exist. The Banking Commission's report he described as a weighty document which seemed to have been put into a refrigerator. Referring to the increase in TDs' allowances, Phelan said it had been stated that even IR£480 was not sufficient to pay a deputy who did his duty, namely to study the views of the constituents. He concluded by saying that "I'm afraid, however, we don't see enough of them."[66]

By early March, the suggestions of the Banking Commission became part of the general discourse in the drafting of general bills, with them becoming an expected practice. An *Irish Independent* article on 'Better Legislation,' regarding the Fisheries Acts, argued that "in referring to new legislation, the Banking Commission made an important recommendation. 'We think,' said the Commission, in its report, 'that it would be of great value, both for members of the Oireachtas and the public, if every Bill containing important or intricate financial clauses were accompanied by an explanatory financial memorandum. This useful practice is adopted elsewhere.' We see no reason why an explanatory memorandum should not accompany Bills of all kinds. We note with satisfaction that the Government had already adopted this practice, for an explanatory memorandum was issued with the Valuation Bill and the Offences Against the State Bill. For some reason, no memorandum was issued

---

[65] *Donegal Democrat 25/2/1939*

[66] *Cork Examiner 28/2/1939*

with the Fisheries Bill. We trust, however, that this is only a temporary lapse and that in future a memorandum will be issued to the public with every Bill."[67]

Meanwhile, at a meeting of Donegal County Council, the 'social credit' campaign, based on the distributist philosophy of Major C.H Douglas came to light on the subject of rates. Heading a delegation on the topic was Mr Frank Gallagher, a well known solicitor in Donegal. Gallagher suggested that the government should create its own credit instead of leaving the burden on ratepayers. Captain John Scott, of Burnstown House, a member of the Donegal County Council, and a prominent unionist and former chair of the Donegal Protestant Registration Association (DPRA), jumped in and posed to Gallagher: "In other words, you want us to become a nation of counterfeiters?"

Gallagher took the opportunity to explain the basics of money and banking and replied by saying "in view of Capt. Scott's interjection, it is very interesting to ask where does the money come from at the present time, when there is no increase in the money supply. At the present time, money is created by the banks every time they make a loan. Your overdraft of £70,000 is not taken from some person's deposit or current account - by the mere act of lending this sum to you it is created and it costs the bank nothing, except the pen, ink and paper."

Scott, still begrudging Gallagher, exclaimed "you try to get an overdraft and you will soon find that out." To this, Gallagher replied "some of you may be slow to believe me when I state this, but I do not ask you to take my word for it. I shall refer you to, and quote some authorities for the proposition that even the most sceptical among you must accept, and that Captain Scott will accept as readily as he would an extract of the Bible. The '*Encyclopaedia Brittanica*' is a standard work that, I am sure, any of you will accept as an undoubted authority

---

[67] *Irish Independent 3/3/1939*

for anything contained in it and it states in Vol. 3, under the heading 'Banking and Credit' that 'banks create credit. It is a mistake to suppose that bank credit is created to any important extent by the payment of money into banks,' and in Vol.15, under the heading 'Money,' - 'Banks lend by creating credit: they create the means of payment out of nothing.'"

Scott, however, was not budging. Instead, he fired back that "you don't say anything about the security behind the credit." Once again, Gallagher replied by citing further sources and stated "I can also refer you to the book, 'Post-War Banking Policy,' by Reginald McKenna, the chairman of one of the biggest joint stock banks in England. The MacMillan Banking Commission Report (page thirty-four) and our own Banking Commission reports, and many other authorities. So now you know where money comes from; the banks create it by writing figures in books, and for every £100 in the country there is about 18s in the tangible form of coin or notes. The rest consists of an abstract for lot of figures in account books called credit, for which coin and notes act as small change. Why hesitate to join with us in calling on the Government to take control of the creation of credit, as recommended in some of our Banking Commission reports? Why should we be the only country in the world that cannot have a credit expansion to suit the requirements of our economic system? Some people say it might upset our system and do harm if the Government took control of the creation of credit. It has not done much harm, but has been of tremendous benefit to New Zealand, Portugal, and several over countries."

Scott claimed Gallagher's proposals were "socialistic ballyhoo, and a fantastic idea of dreamers and will o' the wisps, backed by plausible platitudes to trap the unwary and the gullible." He further added that he regretted that this "egregious business" was not disposed of at a previous meeting, and thereby, have saved a "further waste of time." Scott drew out further criticisms of Gallagher, to which Councillor Kavanagh said to Scott "you will be beaten" and Councillor O'Brien saying "do you think, Councillor Scott, that you own this council?"[68] [69]

A sharp criticism was given of the Valuation Bill at a meeting of the Dublin Corporation at the beginning of March. Mr Byrne claimed that every section of the community would suffer by it, including the occupiers of tenants by way of increased rents. Mr Butler added that villages and towns "through the country deserved overhauling and relief." He claimed that it was "no hardship on any man to be asked to pay just what he should pay." He laid the whole cause for any hardship they suffered by way of slump and depression to the attitude of the banks. He added that the banks were putting into operation the findings of the Banking Commission and were "deliberately restricting credit."[70] He argued that as long as this was allowed to continue, they would have a certain slump in the country.[71]

A review of the March 1939 issue of *The Round Table* by the *Irish Independent* quoted a section of it on industry and agriculture in relation to the questions raised by the Banking Commission. The quote reads;

> *"as the majority report of the Banking Commission points out, the crucial question for Irish industry is whether there will or will not be an improvement in the efficiency of production, on which depends all improvement of the real social income, and thus the standard of living. Technical efficiency, which is particularly important in smaller factories such as exist here, can only be secured by constant vigilance, which the Prices*

---

[68] Donegal News 4/3/1939

[69] Hughs, Brian & Morrissey, Conor (2020). *Southern Irish Loyalism, 1912-1949.* Oxford University Press.

[70] *Evening Herald 7/3/1939*

[71] *Irish Press 7/3/1939*

> *Commission will certainly help to supply Mr Lemass, the Minister for Industry and Commerce, whose speeches are an interesting study in gradual economic education, is apparently alive to these facts, for he recently stated that the next year or two would be the critical period for most of our new industries and that the question whether they were to survive would depend on their quality of their work and the quantity of their output. His former unqualified optimism has recently been considerably modified, and he shows a growing disposition to blame employers, workers and the public for the difficulties that have arisen in the development of his industrial policy. He now claims that if it does not succeed, the Irish people will have been proved unfit for nationhood. It is possible, of course, that it is the policy that is to blame and not the people."*[72]

The subject of reporting the state of the national income appeared in the press at this time, as the *Irish Independent* ran a piece titled 'Prompt Publicity Essential.' The article exhorted that "referring to the necessity for adequate publicity respecting the facts of State finance, the Banking Commission observed that in order that publicity may be adequate, it should not only supply information in a sufficiently detailed degree, but it should do so "before the facts have become so old as to appear no longer to form part of current practical problems." The Commission went on to speak of the delay which takes place after the expiration of the financial year before accounts, or reports of transactions relating to that year are published. It must be admitted that while some Departments endeavour to present their reports with the utmost possible expedition, publication by others is so belated that the facts are so stale as "to form no part of current practical problems." For belatedness of the Revenue Commissioners easily wins first first prize - their latest annual report is for the year ended March 31, 1935. The British Inland Revenue Commissioners have

---

[72] *Cork Examiner 8/3/1939*

just published their report for 1937-1938; and the Report of the British Commissioners of Customs and Excise for the same year was published in December last. The delay on the part of the Revenue Commissioners is unreasonable. The British Inland Revenue Report contains a good deal of material concerning Northern Ireland, which would be valuable for comparison with Eire if the Report of the Revenue Commissioners for the same year were available. A particularly striking Northern item under the head of Income Tax is the actual income, that is the gross income, less exemptions and reductions, from the ownership of houses and lands. The amount was £3,985,271, as compared with £2,832,677 in 1931-32. In the meantime, the revaluation of Northern Ireland had taken place and become operative. Hence the large increase. It has been said that the British Government insisted on the revaluation because it wanted to obtain a larger income tax contribution from Northern Ireland. The returns show how greatly the exchequer has benefited."[73]

At a committee reading of the Trade Loans (Guarantee) Bill, which intended to continue the existing trade loan guarantee system for a further five year period, Senator Professor Johnston described the measure as being "in flat defiance of one of the important recommendations of the Banking Commission." He added that "I do not regard the words uttered by that body as sacrosanct, but it was a body of world renowned experts on whom the State spent £10,000. I think we must consider very carefully all the recommendations before deciding to fly in the face of any one of them."

Lemass, in reply, speaking of the Banking Commission report, said that he agreed with some parts, but that there were some other aspects which irritated him. Of the paragraph quoted by Johnston, dealing with the introduction of measures, including land and housing policies "without a thorough examination of their wider implications from the monetary report of view," he said; "as a matter of fact I think they had

---

[73] *Irish Independent* 8/3/1939

a damned cheek to put down that paragraph. They had no right to assume that no consideration had been given to these aspects of the matter."[74]

At the beginning of April 1939, in review of the income taxation figures for the previous financial year, the Irish Independent claimed that the income tax rate being one shilling above the charge that existed before the Fianna Fáil government correlated the statement of the Banking Commission that the increased proceeds of taxation were due not to a higher yield of a steady level of imposts, but to additions to the imposts themselves. The additions to indirect imposts, it was argued were even more formidable than the increases in direct taxes.[75] On the same day, an edition of the *Republican Review* ran an article titled 'The Tragedy of Unemployment,' subtitled with the phrase 'Our English Housekeeper,' clearly, as displayed in this piece (and in the context of the publication's loyalties), a euphemism for the British Empire. Again penned by Maud Gonne, writing on this 'English housekeeper,' she claims that;

> *"Her scullions on the Banking Commission say that we are extravagant and are spending far too much on Housing and Social Services. They think the unemployed will linger too long if they have a roof over their heads; they would die off quicker if they had only a ditch to shelter them.*
>
> *Poor unemployed! Those who attack the Giant with the Baton are perhaps wiser than those who miserably wail for charitable bones. That is the only alternative so long as we have an English housekeeper. But why should we keep her?*
>
> *We keep the housekeeper because we must, because it is part of our agreement with England that our pound must be tied to*

---

[74] *Irish Press 9/3/1939*

[75] *Irish Independent 1/4/1939*

> *English sterling. It is part of our agreement with England that our unemployed must starve, although the country is rich enough to support nearly twice the present population. And out agreement with England is more binding on the Twenty six County Government than the new 'Constitution' which 'guarantees' that 'the citizens (all of whom, men and women equally, have the right to an adequate means of livelihood, may through their occupations find the means of making reasonable provision for their domestic needs.'*
>
> It is more binding on the Fianna Fáil government than the teachings of Pope Pius XI."

Less than a week later, a warm tribute was paid to the "skill and care" with which the Banking Commission had carried out its immense task was paid by Mr. G. Brock, FCA, President of the Institute of Chartered Accountants in Ireland, when he read a paper on the Report on the Commission at a meeting of the Dublin Society of Chartered Accountants. The capitalisation of industries which had been inaugurated or extended during the past few years, and the improbability of their securing export markets to any extent, because of comparatively low scale production and high internal costs, were among the aspects of the Report dealt with by Brock.[76]

At the impending opening annual conference of the Labour Party, held at the Teachers' Club, Parnell Square, Dublin, the Cork Borough Constituency Council asked that the government be called upon to adopt the principles outlined in the Minority Report of the Banking Commission, which was submitted by Mr. W. O'Brien, Mr. S. Campbell and Professor Alfred O'Rahilly.[77] On 12th April 1939, commending Hitler's creation of a German State Bank, the *Wolfe Tone Weekly*, in an article written by 'Uisneach,' argued that;

---

[76] *Irish Press 6/4/1939*

[77] *Irish Independent 10/4/1939*

"In accordance with the way Hitler's resolutions have of being carried out the German State Bank has been taken over by the Government, and a completely new personnel installed to manage it. The last news of Dr. Schacht, the dismissed head of the State Bank, is that he has gone on a prolonged holiday. Not too bad.

Making the State Bank a "note institution" means that the bank henceforth will issue money to the value of the nation's production of real wealth. The money, therefore, will have as backing goods and services, not gold and foreign exchange (foreign money). Hitler made clear what he intended to do by throwing ridicule on the opinion on the opinion that the validity of money depends on gold and foreign exchange lying in bank vaults; and still greater ridicule on the opinion that the value of money is guaranteed by those things. All of which makes the Banking Commission look exactly like the lump of cheese that it was."[78]

On 1st May 1939, Mr. J.J Walsh, President of the Federation of Irish Manufacturers, appealed for a separate export section attached to the Department of External Affairs to provide information dealing with data on prevailing prices, types of export required, freights, insurance, import regulations, as well as a list of reliable agents, and the provision of financial guarantees for exports to certain countries. He argued that according to the Banking Commission Report, at the final stages of the Economic War, there was, it was stated, a real adverse trade balance after allowing for all invisible exports, of over £3,000,000 per annum. According to recent statistics, this had been reduced, but the position was far from satisfactory, since some of the items of invisible exports could not be counted upon to continue. Walsh claimed that a vicious circle operated, namely, that the Government were unwilling to stimulate exports by special action because the exporters had shown

---

[78] *Wolfe Tone Weekly 12/4/1939*

no special desire to venture into this field. The exporters, in their turn, took this attitude because they lacked very essential machinery for so doing. Trade by barter had allegedly become universal in the world, and governments had literally to enter into business themselves in order to provide markets.[79]

Meanwhile, an issue of the *Republican Review* printed a stirring article by Maud Gonne MacBride titled 'Take Control of Our Credit.' It argued that "money, to fulfil properly its function, must correspond with production, and that credit is simply the belief in the power to produce." Referring to the 1931 encyclical *Quadragessimo anno*, they argue that "the encyclical goes on to say that the money the financiers use is often not their own, and exhorts governments to take control of credit from their hands and use it for the common good." The article criticised the inaction of the government of a country which presented itself to be Catholic, as well as the actions to censor the promotion of the Pope's pronouncements against the existing financial system. It argued that;

> *"The late Pope Pius XI spoke so plainly against the international financiers and bankers, that the Catholic rulers of the Twenty-Six counties don't see it. Translations of Quadragessimo Anno are not popular; hundreds of them being sold at one penny were seized one Sunday morning from the hands of the women who were selling them, and, under the approving eye of the Superintendent of the Fianna Fáil government's police, were solemnly burned outside Our Lady of Lourdes Chapel by some pious but very ignorant members of the congregation."*

It described credit creation through a brief history of the establishment of the Bank of England, and the creation of one million pounds, and that;

---

[79] *Irish Independent* 1/5/1939

> *"one million turned into two at the stroke of a pen. One million not based on production, but on debt, and the operation was repeated many times. The history of the Bank of Ireland, manager of our public debt, is identical. It was founded in 1782 by a loan of £600,000 to the Government, on which it could also issue corresponding paper money based on debt. Debts are the breadth of life to banks, but debts on which interest is paid are millstones on Ireland and are strangling production."*

In her final paragraph, Gonne MacBride, appealing to the sentiments of the time, places a Catholic emphasis on the need for reforms, which are contrasted to the views of Protestant thinking. She writes that;

> *"As we aspire to be a Christian State, we should consider the fight put up for centuries by the Christian Church against usury - defined as any interest exacted for the use of money. The many Canonical Decrees of the Church against usury, as set out in the Catholic Encyclopaedia, have never been rescinded, though in the Nineteenth Century, Calvin's definition that interest on loans is only usury when excessive, seems to be accepted. Interest on debts, at whatever percentage, is excessive when it strangles production and keeps 100,000 of our people unemployed, and why pay for the use of what is our own - the Nation's Credit?"*[80]

Over a week later, John MacDermod of the *Irish Press* stated that the Banking Commission warned that the dead-weight of debt was already too high. The previous year, it was nominally increased by IR£10 million in respect of the financial settlement with Great Britain, but as that settlement released the country from a claim of capital value of about £100 million, its practical effect was that of greatly strengthening our financial position. Borrowing, however, was a

---

[80] *Republican Review* 1/5/1939

practice of which Sean Mac Entee allegedly took a "conservative view." Consequently, it was claimed, he had resorted to it only where it was a case of meeting definitely abnormal charges or requirements of permanent value to the country. At the presenting of the Budget, W.T Cosgrave stated that the Banking Commission had made some striking comparisons in our disfavour between Eire and comparable countries showing that the borrowings of countries like Sweden, Norway and Denmark had created national assets which in some cases yielded an annual profit after paying interest and sinking fund on the debts.[81] The *Irish Independent* reported on 25th May 1939 that it was shown in the Banking Commission that the advances to farmers were distributed over 125,000 borrowers, a large percentage of the total number of land holders. Owing to the abnormal conditions prevailing in the agricultural industry from 1932 onwards, many farmers were unable to meet their obligations to the banks. Owing to the scope of recent land legislation security of tenure is not the valuable asset it had been. It was feared by the Banking Commission that this insecurity of tenure would react on the banks, and on the prospects and terms of future lending for agricultural purposes.[82]

Writing in the June 1939 edition of *The Cork Co-Operator*, Labour's Timothy Quill, the publication's editor, in an article titled *The Money Problem - Some Facts*, focusing on housing loans for the Cork Corporation, criticised the government's inaction on the issue of credit facilities, despite the advice of authoritative figures, and wrote that;

> *"Recently, there has been a good deal said about the control of money, credit and currency. A Commission took evidence on Banking. A majority report and two minority reports were issued. So far, the Government has done nothing in regard to either and is not likely to, until the people see the need for a change, and then demand it...*

---

[81] *Irish Press 11/5/1939*

[82] *Irish Independent 25/5/1939*

Credit Where It's Due: The Money Debate in 1930s Ireland

...Many people fail to realise that with the enormous productive capacity of our industrial system today, it is no longer necessary to work so hard or so long as in former times. In fact, most of the goods required, particularly food and clothing, can now be produced in abundance with less personal toil. Yet there exists poverty in most countries. The real trouble is that money and money power now exceed their rightful use, to serve as a medium of exchange. In reality, money which should simply act like a river to carry the ships containing food from one town down to the next is now more important than the goods it carries. The river refuses to carry the goods down to the next town and the people are poverty stricken. The boots and shoes are in the warehouse in the principal streets. Money prevents them being taken down the side streets or out the country to the shabby and bootless children. The river called 'money,' does not flow sufficiently strong, or enough of it to those places, to help them get the goods. Naturally, one might say, why then does not the Government go in for a proper drainage system to enable the goods to be taken where wanted: It is mainly due to the fact that the people and even the Government have not in the first place got away from the false notion that money is a commodity of intrinsic value. This view continues from the time when it was so and the false notion is fostered by the suggestion that money is inseparable from gold. In the second place, there still exists the false notion that banks do not create money, but only safeguard the deposits of their clients. There also exists a failure to realise the growing rate at which machinery, electricity and steam are replacing man-power and making so much of this physical work superfluous, and the possibility of providing sufficient for all, as a result of the immense possibilities in modern production. To meet the ever present problems of unemployment and poverty, which are causing physical and moral crimes, it is clear that the Government must govern its people and take on its rightful

function of supreme control of the issue of credit and control of the money system, seeing that the real security for credit is the goods produced and services rendered by the people themselves.

In answer to the reply that may be made, that this is state interference, the answer is yes, state interference when necessary. Pope Pius XI declared that there are some economic activities better discharged by the State itself. He says there are some too important to be exposed to the risk of private monopoly to be entrusted to private enterprise."

Concluding, he quoted the Rev. Professor P. Coffey, S.T.L., on monetary policy - "it seems to be a function which should belong exclusively to the State itself, and which never should have been entrusted to the risk of private control, which has actually culminated in an irresponsible and supra-national world monopoly."[83]

In a Dail debate on the 1939 Land Bill, Michael O'Clery of Fianna Fail said that the Bill was greatly needed, because it was "well known for the last three years there would be scarcely any acquisition were it not that the Commission, illegally as now proved, had acquired land on an extensive scale." It was a false doctrine to say that division must be slowed down and people left in land slums and people forced to emigrate because the Banking Commission thought it was not an economic proposition.[84] On 9th June 1939, Fianna Fáil TD for Clare, P.J O'Loghlen, criticised the Rev. E.J Coyne, S.J for an article on the Reports of the Banking Commission, which he had written in an issue of the *Irish Monthly*. O'Loghlen claimed that Coyne had "completely misrepresented the Third Minority Report, of which I was the author." He stated that "perhaps, therefore, it was hardly fair of me to challenge him, if he thought so badly of my proposals, to produce

---

[83] *The Cork Co-Operator - June 1939 edition*

[84] *Irish Press 8/6/1939*

better ones of his own. In any event, he has not produced them. If he has any constructive proposals which would enable us to end unemployment and bring about a juster social order, it is a pity that he has confined himself hitherto to condemning other men's proposals while producing none of his own."[85]

Speaking on the Banking Report in a Day debate, the Taoiseach, Eamon de Valera, stated that if deputies wanted a full dress debate on the Banking Commission report or the question of credit, they would have it. He believed in certain fundamental principles in regard to social economics and the only regret he had with regard to the Banking Commission report was that some of the questions which should have been put in for early discussion were only put in at the end. As far as the Government was concerned, the principles that were enunciated in the third minority report as social principles there admitted them and agreed to them, but it was quite a different thing to admit general principles and fundamental principles, and then to accept some particular scheme which was put forward and was said to be in line with these principles as a practical and good solution. They claimed that had to deal with it from a "practical point of view." Fine Gael's James Dillon complained that P.J O'Loghlen, in his minority report as a member of the Banking Commission, appeared to have been fascinated and dominated by the "New Zealand experiment" and all his recommendations ran largely on the lines of that plan, which had now gone "bust." The Government's policy generally came under attack from several speakers, with Dillon declaring that the banks here were choked with Government "paper." There were several references to individual Ministers and the Ceann Comhairle had to frequently intervene.[86]

---

[85] *Irish Press 9/6/1939*

[86] *Irish Press 15/6/1939*

Take Control of Our Credit

IN a recent issue of the *Wolfe Tone Weekly* an article entitled "Republic or Plutocracy" by "Uisneach," shows in clear plain language that money, to fulfil properly its function, must correspond with production, and that credit is simply the belief in the power to produce.

He said that National Credit is the sum total of the credit of individual producers of the nation. He then showed that the Bank of England has been allowed, as Central Bank of Ireland, to usurp the control of our Credit—on which our production depends, and which

Credit For The Common Good.

Common Good.—blk. u. and l.

He quoted from that great indictment of the present financial and social system, *Quadragessimo Anno*:

"Domination is most powerfully exercised by those who because they hold and control money also govern credit and determine its allotment, for that reason supplying, so to speak, the life blood to the entire economic body and grasping in their hands, as it were, the very soul of production, so that no one can breathe against their will."

The Encyclical goes on to say that the money they (the financiers) use, *is often not their own*, and exhorts governments to take this control of credit from their hands and use it for the common good.

Solemnly Burned.

The late Pope Pius XI. spoke so plainly against the international financiers and bankers that the Catholic rulers of the Twenty-Six Counties don't see it. Translations of *Quadragessimo Anno* are not popular; hundreds of them being sold at one penny were seized one Sunday morning from the hands of the women who were selling them and, under the approving eye of a Superintendent of the Fianna Fáil Government's police, were solemnly burned outside Our Lady of Lourdes Chapel by some pious but very ignorant members of the congregation.

Hitler—although he is a Dictator enforcing a system of government with which Republicans do not agree—does not think, like Mr.

Seán MacEntee, that finance is too complicated for the German people to understand.

On the contrary, he explained it to the deputies of the German Reich, and caused his speech to be broadcast to the people. He said that German finance—money and credit—was based on production and not on international finance and usury. Through this he was able to boast that every one of the seven millions of unemployed he found on taking office, was now a wage earner. There is no unemployment, no half time, no slowing down of production in Germany.

The Bank of England.

Consider for a moment International Finance from which Germany is escaping, and from which Republicans hope, with the blessing of God, Ireland will also one day escape.

Take our Central Bank, the Bank of England, as an example. Any one who cars can read its history in the National Library.

It was founded in 1694 by some financiers who lent one million pounds at 8 per cent. interest to the King of England. They were authorised by charter to issue another million in paper money to lend also at interest, on the security of the King's *Debt*.

One million turned into two at the stroke of a pen. One million *not based on production but on debt*, and the operation was repeated many times.

The history of the Bank of Ireland, manager of our public debt, is identical. It was founded in 1782 by a loan of £600,000 to the Government on which it could also issue corresponding paper money based on debt.

Debts are the breath of life to banks but debts on which interest is paid are millstones on Ireland and are strangling production.

We, like Germany, must increase production if we would increase the wellbeing of our people, and enable them to live free from debt and from anxiety.

Our task is easier than Germany's because we have more than sufficient land for our requirements. She has only one acre for every 135 persons which forces her to import many of the necessaries

complicated for the German people of life. But she controls her own credit and we fools are leaving ours to the control of the Bank of England. Our credit is being used for English war production instead of for Irish industry and agricultural development. Our farmers, on whom the entire nation depends, are bound down by debt and discouragement. Every note we use must be backed by British War Loan—a fact which every one knows but which Mr. MacEntee says we are not capable of understanding.

Excessive Interest.

As we aspire to be a Christian State we should consider the fight put up for centuries by the Christian Church against usury—defined as *any* interest exacted for the use of money. The many Canonical Decrees of the Church against usury, as set out in the Catholic Encyclopedia, have never been rescinded, though in the Nineteenth Century Calvin's definition that interest on loans is only usury when excessive, seems to be accepted.

Interest on debts, at whatever percentage, is excessive when it strangles production and keeps 100,000 of our people unemployed, and why pay for the use of what is our own—the Nation's Credit?

—M.G.

WISE AND OTHERWISE

(Continued from Page 8.)

15. Said Mr. Chamberlain in the British House of Commons: "I can assure the hon. member that there are no ideological difficulties between ourselves and Soviet Russia." We always thought there was something fundamental which prevented Ireland from associating with England. Now we know. Henry VIII. started Bolshevism, Stalin carried it on, and Chamberlain is going to take up where Stalin leaves off. Nice friends de Valera chooses for himself.

* * *

16. Is Aiken a pain? Join the army and find out.

AN EXAMPLE OF AN ARTICLE WRITTEN BY MAUD GONNE MACBRIDE IN THE RADICAL 'REPUBLICAN REVIEW' NEWSPAPER (1939)

The national executive of the 'National Association of Old IRA,' headed by its president, Simon O'Donnghaile, put forward its own proposal for financial reform. They argued that;

> *"No nation in the world is in monetary and economic subordination to another country as Ireland is to England. Mr de Valera maintains this economic subordination, just as Mr Cosgrave did and on the same advice. We repeat, that Ireland alone among the nations of the world has no national monetary system; her rigid attachment to English sterling (England's paper £1) integrates her in helpless economic subordination to the Bank of England and the British Treasury. No Government of Ireland will be able to employ the 100,000 unemployable adults of the 26 counties until Ireland has full control of her own monetary system. No Government of Ireland will be able to provide employment for the 90,000 unemployed of the Six Counties until we have financial autonomy.*
>
> *Therefore, the monetary subordination to England, which Mr de Valera maintains on the advice of those officials who contributed so much to the disastrous course of the previous Government, is an actual barrier to the removal of partition. Your reference to Denmark as having deliberately decided to link the currency with the sterling group, shows either a grossly inadequate knowledge of economic and monetary facts of the last few years, or else a wilful attempt to keep them from the knowledge of the public. In 1933, Denmark re-adjusted her exchange to a deliberate disparity with sterling, to the same degree of New Zealand. This gave great benefit to the rural communities of both countries. New Zealand agricultural exports obtain £125 for every £100 they sell in the British market. Denmark has no rigid attachment to sterling; she re-adjusts her rate of exchange as the national*

needs require, while Ireland is being ground to pieces by her English monetary system.

The National Executive has proposed a monetary policy which has the same underlying economic and monetary principles as the successful adjustments of New Zealand and Portugal, namely, that the volume of money (currency and credits) must be adjusted to maintain full economic activity and full employment, at proper wages, on constructive work of national importance. The same economic and monetary principle is continued in Minority Report III of the Banking Commission.

It is useless for Ministers and others to say that no constructive proposals to end unemployment have been put before them. The plain fact is that Mr de Valera and his Ministers will not examine the proposals we have made - and the constructive monetary policy essential to national freedom, and family security, is left to the considerations of those same officials and expert advisers who have already brought the previous Government to ruin, and who will bring both Ireland and Mr de Valera to ruin if permitted.'[87]

Discussing 'Incomes and Savings,' an *Irish Independent* feature dismissed the 'tax the rich' mentality, the writer complained that the decline in national income in recent years, as had been noted by the Banking Commission, had been accompanied by a "stupendous and wholly indefensible increase in taxation." They argued that this was not the way to encourage the investment of private capital in enterprises.[88] In a letter to the editor of the *Irish Press*, penned by Mr. T.F Harvey Jacob, while agreeing with the economist Mr. T. Kennedy that "a good deal of confused and misinformed thinking and speaking

---

[87] *Irish Press* 17/6/1939

[88] *Irish Independent* 20/6/1939

prevails on this subject," he dismissed the promotion of the distributist 'social credit,' economic theory, and stating that the 'A plus B' theorem, a core element of the ideology, is a "fallacious argument, because it treats industry as though it operated in spasms, or closed periods of time, instead of as a continuous flow."[89]

Additionally, the conclusions of the Banking Commission angered a close personal friend of Eamon de Valera, the Rev. Fr. Edward J. Cahill, SJ, a prominent figure in Irish society who founded the 'An Ríoghacht' group. According to Dr. Thomas J. Morrissey, in his 2016 book *The Ireland of Edward Cahill SJ*, Cahill would become a vociferous opponent of the commission's proposals. The Banking system, in the mind of Cahill and An Ríoghacht, existed to "serve the people." Consequently, they believed, the social needs of the citizens had to be reflected in the country's economic and banking system. The brief given regarding the Banking Commission appeared to allow for this, and An Ríoghacht saw the inquiry as an opportunity to have the Papal social principles applied to peoples' needs. It is important, therefore, to view the terms of reference given to the Commission, which were as follows;

> *"To examine and report on the system in Saorstát Éireann of currency, banking, credit, public borrowing and lending and the pledging of State Credit on behalf of agriculture, industry, and the social services, and to consider and report what changes, if any, are necessary or desirable to promote the social and economic welfare of the community and the interests of agriculture and industry."*

This was of particular interest to Cahill. He actively campaigned for the opportunity for both him and An Ríoghacht to be given input into the formation of the Commission's views, largely without success. Following the publication of the Commission's reports, An Ríoghacht

---

[89] *Irish Press 27/6/1939*

were extremely disappointed at the tendency of a majority of the commissioners towards a conservative outcome, which they believed was neglectful of social reform. Eoin O'Keeffe, a member of An Ríoghacht and another life-long friend of de Valera, approached the Taoiseach and expressed his annoyance that the report of the Commission would simply endorse the existing fiscal theory and practice of the Department of Finance. Fr Edward Coyne, SJ, writing in an issue of *Studies*, stated that the Commission had made a serious error in omitting post-war economic thinking, including that of John Maynard Keynes. As a result, he feared that the Majority Report would "come to be regarded as a museum piece."

An Ríoghacht instead published 2,000 copies of its own report, much to the annoyance of the Department of Finance, which became alarmed at the popularity that the minority reports seemed to enjoy among the public in general and the Fianna Fáil party in particular. It went to extraordinary lengths to discredit the origins of the minority reports. One submission to the government cabinet highlighted the similarity between the First and Third Minority Reports and both the Labour Party programme of 1938 and the economic proposals of the Anti-Treaty IRA. Through both the An Ríoghacht and Muintir na Tire organisations, Cahill would become a high profile critic of the type of financial system supported by the commission and the government in the late 1930s and early 1940s.[90]

---

[90] Morrissey, T.J. (2016). *The Ireland of Edward Cahill SJ, 1868-1941*. Messenger Publications.

Credit Where It's Due: The Money Debate in 1930s Ireland

THE CENTRAL BANK ACT

In March 1941, the Taoiseach, Mr. Eamon de Valera, announced that the Government had decided to introduce legislation to establish a central bank, which directed attention to the opinion of the Banking Commission on the subject in its 1938 majority report. The commission recommended an increase in the banking functions of the Currency Commission, to comprise, in effect, the range of functions which a central bank suited to Ireland would exercise. The report stated that the principal duty of the Bank, should be to maintain the "integrity of the national monetary unit." The maintenance of external currency stability, which was one of the main functions of a central bank, was supervised by the Currency Commission to the extent of the link with the Sterling Exchange. The report also recommended that no attempt should be made to build up a money market in Dublin on the basis of issue of Treasury Bills, and that the greatest care should be taken with regard to the issue of such Bills by the Government. It was further emphasised by the commission that any powers granted to a monetary authority to re-discount bills, or make advances against the collateral of Government securities to other credit institutions, should be used only "in exceptional circumstances."[91]

Mr. Sean T. O'Kelly, Fianna Fáil's Minister for Finance, announced in the Seanad in July 1941 that a central bank bill was "practically drafted," in reply to the debate on the Final Stage of the Finance Bill, which was passed. O'Kelly stated that;

> *"Except for a few croakers, wailers and snivelers, the country has come through the past nine years with flying colours, and we will stand up well to the dangers and difficulties that are pressuring us on all sides today, under the present leadership,*

---

[91] *Irish Independent 21/3/1941*

in which the country has complete confidence and which has been tested time and again."[92]

In February 1942, the annual report of the National Agricultural and Industrial Development Association (NAIDA) stated that the outcome of the proposals for an Irish Central Bank was awaited with considerable anxiety by its membesrs. It claimed that housing, afforestation, land, and bog drainage and construction of national aerodromes could not be tackled on any adequate scale, if the necessary capital had to be borrowed even at moderate rates of interest, as such undertakings were thus loaded from the beginning with an almost un-payable burden of financial debt.[93] By early March, the Central Bank Bill (1942) had been introduced. Writing in a feature article in the *Irish Press*, Mr. Liam O'Buachalla, M.Comm, stated that;

"The Central Bank Bill (1942) has been introduced at last. Some people have been impatiently demanding it. The rest, realising more fully perhaps, the extent and importance of the subject matter which it was intended it should cover, were not at all anxious that its preparation should be rushed.

The establishment of a Central Bank was recommended in the Banking Commission's (1938) Report. The Commission, consisting of twenty-one members, issued its reports in March, 1938, approximately four years after its appointment. The Majority Report carried the signatures of sixteen of the Commissioners, the remaining five, while differing from the majority, also differed among themselves, such differences being reflected in the issue of three Minority Reports, one of which carried three signatures...

---

[92] *Irish Press 17/7/1941*

[93] *Irish Press 2/2/1942*

While waiting to see the text of the Central Bank Bill, it might be as well to consider for a moment what a Central Bank is. As to pattern, there is no standard. The Bank of England is, however, usually taken as the most outstanding example. In the matter of aims, one might say there is unanimity. The outstanding aim is to control banking and currency in such a way as to promote the monetary policy of the State. Obviously, this monetary policy must concern itself, mainly, with the regulation of the quantities of circulating medium so as to ensure, in the best interests as a whole, the most advantageous functioning and development of the country's industry and trade. Pari passu with this aim, a close eye must be kept on the balance of payments. In other words, a sound monetary policy must always aim at securing and maintaining at the highest level possible what is usually referred to as the 'integrity of the national monetary unit.'

Let us now consider, even though very briefly, after an examination of the structure and procedure of various Central Banks, what are the powers a Central Bank should have in order to carry out as completely and as effectively as may be, the fundamental business entrusted to it by tradition, or, as is more generally the case, by the government."

The most importance functions of the bank listed by O'Buachalla included its complete control of the Note issue, the power to re-discount bills of exchange and to make advances against bills and government securities, its possession of the power to buy and sell government securities, as well as to be in a position to bring about changes in the interest rates.[94]

On 12 March, 1942, William Norton, Michael J. Keyes and William Davin, all Labour TDs, asked the Dáil to refuse the Central Bank Bill a

---

[94] *Irish Press 5/3/1942*

second reading on the grounds that it does not provide that the monetary authority will be amenable to the Oireachtas, as well as containing no provision for removing the limitation on the issue of currency by the Irish monetary authority imposed by the Currency Act (1927). Furthermore, they complained that it was not possible for the Bank, within the Bill, to safeguard the currency's integrity or promote the whole people's welfare, and that the Bill fails to provide for the promotion of such re-organisation of the economy as to enable the Government "to provide full employment at proper wages for the thousands out of work, cause a cessation of involuntary emigration, put an end to poverty and enable the people in rural Ireland to derive a decent livelihood from the efficient cultivation of the land."[95]

A fortnight later, Sean T. O'Kelly (Minister for Finance) spoke in strong support of the Bill and the functions of the proposed central bank, stating that;

> *"As a result of the merging of the note reserve fund with the general fund, and acceptance of deposits from commercial banks, the new Central Bank would have at its disposal much larger resources than the Currency Commission as a basis on which to conduct open market operations...*
>
> *A central bank which has the power of open market operations is equipped with a potent instrument for controlling and regulating credit and this will be one of the powers of our proposed Central Bank...*
>
> *The external position is safeguarded by having a sufficient of external assets in the Legal Tender Note Fund to meet any unfavourable turn in the balance of payments. Almost every central bank throughout the world is compelled to have a minimum of gold, foreign exchange, or other foreign assets to*

---

[95] *Irish Press 12/3/1942*

provide for such a contingency. The internal position depends on a variety of circumstances, but mainly on the price level. So far as purely monetary powers can regulate internal conditions, the Central Bank will have such powers."

The Government argued that it was desirable that the banks should increase their investments within the State, having regard to their relatively large holdings of external, compared with internal, assets. They also claimed that the constant and predominant aim of the new Bank was to be "the welfare of the whole people."

In response, Richard Mulcahy called the proposed central bank one of the "carrots" of Fianna Fáil, claiming that, in fact, it was "carrot number six."[96]

Near the end of the month, the Council of the Federation of Irish Manufacturers discussed the report of a committee which examined the Central Bank Bill. Members agreed that "while the Bill creates no fundamental change of a kind which will affect the interests of industry, machinery has been set up which will enable the people to make any changes in the credit structure considered desirable."

Meanwhile, the Council of the National Agricultural and Industrial Development Association also criticised the bill. In a statement, it said that;

"This Bill is quite worthless as far as making the Irish financial system independent to foreign control, and that system will continue to fail to represent the real ability of Ireland to support and provide a decent livelihood for its citizens."[97]

---

[96] *Irish Press* 26/3/1942

[97] *Irish Press* 30/3/1942

In late April of 1942, the Taoiseach, Mr. Eamon de Valera, speaking in a Dáil debate on the Central Bank Bill, claimed that the Government had never been prevented as a government from carrying out any "worthwhile scheme because of money." He stated that the considerable sums advanced to industry which were lost owing to the fact that the condition under with the work had to be done did not make a return possible. The advances to which he referred to were made under the Trade Loans Acts and not, as had been previously confused, the Industrial Credit Corporation.[98]

In early May, 1942, Professor J. Busteed, M.Comm, Dean of the Faculty of Commerce, UCC, as well as being a member of the Banking Commission, gave a lecture to the Cork Chamber of Commerce, at which Mr. C.F Murphy, president of the Chamber, presided. The lecture was on the topic of "Central Banking, with special reference to its proposed operation in Ireland." Speaking, Busteed stated that;

> *"After the last war, a very large number of new nations or types of government came into existence. They were all full of the spirit of establishing themselves as national entities. They said that their economies had been neglected under previous controls, and that so long as they had a central bank, they could control the financial affairs of their new nations, and as a result become very much richer; but eventually they found that while the establishment of these institutions were desirable, they were not going to provide a panacea for their economic difficulties...*
>
> *In what way could a central bank carry out the activities that would be expected of it? A central bank could not pretend to possess these essentials at all, unless it had the power in a large way, in an important way, to create and destroy credit. It should be able to create or destroy credit to such an extent*

---

[98] *Irish Press* 25/4/1942

> *that it would have an important influence on the general credit position of the country. Around these words a central bank must evolve. In practice, the power of the Bank of England depended largely on the trust that the ordinary interests reposed in it.*
>
> *There were other powers that it was considered a central bank should have - monopoly of the note issue and control of the gold reserve. A central bank should have the power of accepting deposits, but it should not be in competition with the other banks... The setting up of a government in Dublin did not make the slightest change in the credit structure here."*

Referring to the Central Bank Bill, he expressed the view that it would have no power at all over the price of credit, or the volume of credit, or the direction in which credit was to be distributed in the country. The policy of the Bill, he said, was to keep the bank "entirely within the banking structure proper." Concluding, Busteed declared that;

> *"The economy of the nation will have to be shared between private enterprise and the Government. This idea of monetary control from a central authority is a very modern one, and it is going to produce no utopia. It seems that our central bank will not have Government business. The powers to be given to it are not sufficient to make it effective, and even if it had full powers, it would be unwise that it should have a big influence here because of the position of our banks. It would have to be gradual, and of course a lot will depend on the outcome of the war."*[99]

Discussing the Central Bank Bill in late May, 1942, the Taoiseach, Mr. Eamon de Valera, said that he thought that he had pointed out that the central bank's control "would not be coercive, but must have the

---

[99] *Irish Press* 13/5/1942

character of leadership, with co-operation between the central bank, the commercial banks and the Government in regard to the policy that would best serve the country's interests as a whole." He further claimed that the general policy of the central bank in England and other countries, on account of the character of their leadership and prestige, had been followed because it was felt that the people directing that policy had the closest contact with the Government, and with industrial and commercial conditions, and were men whose ability to judge in these matters was respected. They hoped when the Irish central bank was set up, that there would be such good results from co-operation between the Government on one hand, the commercial banks on the other, and the directors of the central bank, that the policy decided by the central bank would be carried out.

In response, General Richard Mulcahy, of Fine Gael, stated that the leadership of the new Bank should be by way of suggestion on part of the Minister for Finance and the Government.[100]

In July 1942, the debate on the Report Stage of the Central Bank on the matter of hire purchase was discussed. Mulcahy said that he did not know of any Central Bank which had any responsibility to look after the business of hire purchase. James Dillon, at that time an Independent TD, said what they were young to do was to provide that the system, which in itself, was not abused. Fine Gael's Henry Morgan Dockrell, TD for Dublin County, said that there were abuses of the system which called legitimately for Government interference. They were "passing the buck," he said, to the central bank. Sean T. O'Kelly, the Minister for Finance, said the majority Report of the Banking Commission had recommended that the Central Bank be empowered to investigate the hire purchase system, strictly confining its inquiry to the "inflationary monetary system."[101]

---

[100] *Irish Press 22/5/1942*

[101] *Irish Independent 11/7/1942*

In October 1942, the Central Bank Bill passed through the Report and Final Stages in the Seanad. Speaking on the topic, Michael Hayes, a Fine Gael Senator, claimed that anyone who thought that the new Central Bank would solve their agricultural or social problems was "making a mistake." Senator James McGee, an Independent, stated that the Bill did not meet the need which the Banking Commission was set up to investigate. Sir John Keane stated that the banks had "nothing to do with the re-orientation of national policy."

The Fianna Fáil government minister, Sean T. O'Kelly, replying, said the Central Bank would be a useful instrument in the hands of a Government "and even an essential instrument in the case of a crisis that might occur when the (Second World) War ended or even before it ended." He also claimed that he was glad to note that despite the strong objections he had taken to certain sections of the Bill, Sir John Keane had promised on behalf of the bankers that they were prepared to co-operate to make the new organisation successful.[102]

Following the passing of the Act, on 1 February 1943, the Currency Commission was officially dissolved. The Central Bank of Ireland is established with particular powers and functions, the most important of which is "safeguarding the integrity of the currency" and, echoing a phrase from Article 45 of the State's Constitution, ensuring that "in what pertains to the control of credit the constant and predominant aim shall be the welfare of the people as a whole." However, certain functions regarded in other countries as characteristic of central banks were not assigned to the Central Bank:

- It did not acquire custody of the cash reserves of the commercial bank.
- The Bank of Ireland retained its position as banker to the government.

---

[102] *Irish Independent 15/10/1942*

- The new institution had no statutory power to restrict credit, though it could promote its expansion (the conditions for influencing credit by open-market operation did not exist).
- Ireland's external monetary reserves continued to be held largely in the form of the external assets of the Associated (i.e., clearing) Banks – the former shareholding banks in the Currency Commission.

President of Ireland, Douglas Hyde, on the advice of the Government, appointed Dr Joseph Brennan as Governor for a statutory 7-year term. He presided over an eight member board of directors. Richard T. McGuinness, former Secretary to the Currency Commission, became Secretary to the Board. The Central Bank's headquarters was established in Foster's Place, Dublin, in the former offices of the Currency Commission.[103]

---

[103] *A Chronology of Main Developments in the Central Bank of Ireland (2013). [online] Available at: https://www.centralbank.ie/docs/default-source/publications/the-history-of-the-central-bank-1943-2013.pdf?sfvrsn=8*

CONCLUSION

The Central Bank of Ireland, like its predecessor, the Currency Commission, has played a leading role in the shaping of the country since its formal establishment in February 1943, including the Great Recession of 2008, the 2020 pandemic-induced recession and their fall-out from both. Despite this, very little material is available on the circumstances and public feeling surrounding its creation. For any student of history, economics, commerce or finance in Ireland, this is a regrettable position. This work, albeit its rather compact nature, has sought to address this issue.

Being born in 2002, by the age of 18, I had grown up through two major, global recessions. As a product of that generation, it is then perhaps natural for me to take an interest in this subject matter. Economies and livelihoods across the globe have been assailed in that period, and the solutions to the causes and effects of these colossal downturns are sought. Although this work is non-partisan in nature and is only intended to explore this often forgotten element of Irish history, for those with an interest in commentary on this, as well as proposed solutions, I would like to draw your attention to the works of several renowned economists of this century, such as (but not limited to) Joseph Stiglitz, Robert Skidelsky, Stephanie Kelton, Larry Randall Wray, Ann Pettifor, Mark Blyth, Sir Paul Collier and Josh Ryan-Collins.

Anyone with an awareness of the most pressing problems in Ireland knows that there is a crisis in this country, a crisis of liquidity for the masses. For example, the surge in the prominence of approved housing bodies (on one of which I serve as a voluntary director) in Ireland via the mortage-to-rent scheme, as well as the general population's dependence on moneylenders (many of whom are illegal and charge interest rates of up to 600%), reveals the pervasive personal debt epidemic that is present in this country. A shortage of money in the pockets of workers, families, and all those who seek employment, those who struggle to pay for their mortgages, education, health and social care, while the deteriorating assets of this country play second fiddle to the desires of private money power, clearly displays that there is an urgent need for a fundamental change in how we deal with the economic problems of today.

You will not support this sentiment if you are satisfied with matters as they stand. If you are eager in allowing this country to simply fall into catastrophe, you must first take heed of the perilous condition in which our economy finds itself. We must not make an erroneous decision in this period. Across this country, shop fronts lie vacant, unused land remains wastefully untilled, idle vehicles rot, industrial estates are swamped by nettles, and milking parlours sit in neglect, as a shortage of money for productive purposes inhibits their use and potential for prosperity. A sad story of financial hardship is behind each and every one of these instances.

For the solution to these problems, credit power ought to be harnessed into full employment and maximised output in every city, town and village in the land, and then, and only then, can an equitable Irish society be realised.

ABOUT THE AUTHOR

At the age of 22 (as of 2024), Tadgh Quill-Manley is an honours BA graduate in Economics & Philosophy from University College Cork (UCC), and concurrently completed the Qualified Financial Advisor (QFA), Certified Insurance Practitioner (CIP), a Pension Trustee Practitioner (PTP) and Certificate in Credit Union Operations (CUA/CUC/CUC), for which he received the Insurance Institute of Ireland's CJ Gladstone High Achiever Award. In university, he served on the committee of the UCC Economics Society. Tadgh is now studying to become a barrister-at-law at the King's Inns, Dublin City, Ireland.

At such a young age, Tadgh Quill-Manley has already served as a volunteer board member of the National Adult Literacy Agency, National Advocacy Service (for People with Disabilities & Patient Advocacy Service), the Irish Horse Welfare Trust, the Irish Council for Social Housing (the national federation of Approved Housing Bodies), the Equine Stakeholders Group (a statutory council at the Department of Agriculture, Food & the Marine, Chaired by the Chief Veterinary Officer), the Munster Agricultural Society (a Seanad nominating body), Chairman of the Irish Architectural Archive's lay Community Advisory Group (CAG), and on the council of the AHEAD Disability Advisory Group.

Locally, he has also served as a volunteer board member of Cork City Childcare Company, Cork City Music College, Cork Craft & Design, Dance Cork-Firkin Crane, Cork Deaf Association, Cork Centre for Independent Living, Employability Cork, Cork Textiles Network, Carbery Housing Association (a Cork city & county-wide Approved Housing Body), and the Council of the Insurance Institute of Cork. In addition, he as served on the Secretariat of the Cork County Public Participation Network (as per Local Government Act, 2013), and as hon. Secretary of Christian Brothers' College, Cork (i.e., CBC, known colloquially as 'Christians'). In all of the aforementioned bodies (both regional and national), he is the youngest ever person to serve on these. In his local community, he has also served as hon. Secretary of Inniscarra Community Centre, hon. Treasurer of Inniscarra Agricultural Show, and on the management committees of Clogheen-Kerrypike Community Association, as well as Blarney-Dawstown Point-to-Point.

He has served on the Executive Board and central council of the Irish Labour Party (on an ex-officio basis), and as chairperson of Labour Youth (previously serving as Policy & Education Officer), as well as chairperson of both the UCC Labour Society and the Labour Youth Cork branch.

Tadgh Quill-Manley is a former National Equitation Champion. Furthermore, he is a facile writer and creator, and, as a youth, winner of several awards in films/documentary/screenplays, including at the 2015 Ireland's Young Filmmaker of the Year Awards. Poetry published in several magazines and journals. Winner of Best Screenplay at Philadelphia Youth Film Festival 2020, shortlisted for same at Beverly Hills International Film Festival at the age of 18 (2020). He has served as a freelance contributor to *Lee Valley Outlook, UCC Economics Journal, That's Farming, Social Europe, The Left Tribune, The Evening Echo* and *The Irish Field* (the latter also including Cheltenham preview specials consecutively in 2022 & 2023).

At the age of 22, he has already published three history books, which currently are:

- *A History of Workers Co-operation in the British Industrial Revolution (2021)*
- *Credit Where It's Due: The Money Debate in 1930s Ireland (2022)*
- *'Til the Cows Come Home: A History of the Cork Farmers' Union (2024)*

Credit Where It's Due: The Money Debate in 1930s Ireland

AUTHOR IN 2021

www.ingramcontent.com/pod-product-compliance
Lightning Source LLC
Chambersburg PA
CBHW071413210526
45465CB00001B/369